On Camera

How to Earn Money in TV Commercials and Other Media

Dwight Weist and
Robert Barron

Walker and Company ☀ New York

First published in the United States of America in 1982 by the Walker Publishing Company, Inc.

Published simultaneously in Canada by John Wiley & Sons Canada, Limited, Rexdale, Ontario.

ISBN: 0-8027-0710-6 (cloth)
      0-8027-7195-5 (paperback)

Book design by Laura Ferguson
Library of Congress Catalog Card Number: 81-70334
Printed in the United States of America

10 9 8 7 6 5 4 3 2 1

Library of Congress Cataloging in Publication Data
Weist, Dwight.
  On camera.

  Includes index.
    1. Acting for television—Vocational guidance.
2. Television advertising—Vocational guidance.
I. Barron, Robert. II. Title.
PN1992.8.A3W4   1982   791.45′028′02373   81-70334
ISBN 0-8027-0710-6
ISBN 0-8027-7195-5 (pbk.)

Contents

Foreword

In 1953 Bob Barron, then a director-producer of commercials for the advertising firm of N. W. Ayer, was holding auditions for a Breck shampoo commercial in a New York studio. One of the auditionees was Dwight Weist. Barron was impressed with Weist's professional, "nonactorish" delivery of the text. Weist was impressed with Barron's clear, succinct directions. After the audition, Barron said, "I've been teaching some classes in commercials for models, and I've been thinking of starting a school. How would you like to be my partner?" And so began a school that has been in existence for twenty-five years, as of the present writing.

In his capacity as producer-director, Bob Barron had long recognized the need in the industry for a school that would teach performing TV commercials. Most of the actors Barron had auditioned were unaware of the difference between "acting" and selling," and the models he had been teaching at the outset could not even read lines and make them sound natural.

Together Bob Barron and Dwight Weist drew up a curriculum and wrote a textbook incorporating the techniques of "acting for television" which they had formulated. The successes of their students soon brought hundreds of students to their doors; not only actors and models, but also singers, teachers, lawyers, policemen, and, of course, housewives, with over a thousand attending classes each year in five video-equipped studios.

The Weist-Barron School is now international, with branches in Atlanta, Philadelphia, Detroit, Los Angeles, Dallas, and Toronto, Canada, and is expanding every year.

Realizing that the New York school and its six branches could not even begin to reach the thousands of people throughout the country who had the potential of becoming effective peformers in commercials, Barron and Weist adapted their textbook into this book to make it available to everyone interested in doing commercials and earning money in this very lucrative field.

It is almost general knowledge that many performers are being paid extremely well for their services on national commercials. Individual income often runs into the hundreds of thousands of dollars a year. What is not as well known is that there are opportunities to earn a good income both in commercials filmed for *local* clients and many other local communications projects. The list is impressive:

- Commercials filmed or taped for local accounts, such as banks, department stores, specialty stores, automobile dealers, restaurants; announcements of local functions; political announcements at election time
- Commercials of all the above performed live at local television or cable stations
- Radio commercials for all of the above
- Industrial films, made at local plants or factories
- Training films—for example, for personnel of companies to improve functioning on their jobs, for salespeople to improve selling techniques
- Slide films (similar to training films, but using still pictures)
- Films made for special exhibits
- Film narration: the voice you hear on travelogues, documentaries, education films, etc.
- Educational films for local schools, colleges, hospitals, etc.
- Modeling, both for print (photographs) and commercials
- Jingles, the catchy tunes sung on commercials.

This book is designed to teach you how to perform in commercials and other film work, how to audition, how and where to seek employment once you have learned the techniques.*

We believe that any intelligent person with an outgoing personality can be taught to do commercials. But this does not always result in instant success. The field abounds with seasoned performers and recognized old pros, yet new faces are constantly in demand. A new face, yes, but a new face alone, however distinctive, is not enough. Many thousands of dollars are spent in preparing and recording commercials. The ad agencies and local TV stations, therefore, are not looking for rank amateurs who do not know their business.

If you study this book well, practice faithfully, and devote time

---

*Since this book is designed to be instructive to both the performer who hopes to make a career in the major production areas and one who will seek employment in a local area, some of the information will not apply to both. As an example, agents and casting directors may not always be present in local areas.

trying to make contacts with both agents and producers (known in the trade as "making the rounds"), a whole new career, either full- or part-time, could open up for you. You will never know unless you give it a try.

Even if you have no desire to do commercials, we believe that this book will give you a fascinating insight into the commercial field in general and will provide you with many helpful hints for your daily life. You will discover as you read that much of the book deals with "communication," and the techniques involved in reading and personal presentation have a much wider application than just learning commercial acting. When you learn how to be a good "communicator," you can increase your earning capacity, no matter what your business or profession.

About the Authors

Dwight Weist is one of the deans of radio and television personalities, for his career spans forty years and includes numerous imposing credits. Mr. Weist recently completed six years as president of the New York branch of the Screen Actors Guild, and for twenty years was a member of that organization's national board. For seventeen years, he was the announcer for *Search for Tomorrow*, a "soap" seen daily on CBS. He spent thirteen years as a regular on radio's *The March of Time*, doing impersonations of world-famous personalities. And thirteen may be his lucky number; he was the narrator of Pathe News for that many years as well. He narrated two feature films: *The Golden Age of Comedy* and *When Comedy Was King*, and was heard as a regular member of the cast of *Buck Rogers* in the role of Tallan of Jupiter. He played Commissioner Weston in *The Shadow*, opposite Orson Welles.

On television, Weist has been highly visible in a battery of commercials, the longest-running of which were Sominex (seven years) and Pepto-Bismol (five years). For many years he was the master of ceremonies of television's *We the People*.

Robert Barron was born into the theater. His father, Enrico Baroni, was a well-known opera singer in the 1920s. His mother, Marion Weeks, was a vaudeville headliner, star of early silent films and talkies, and later a Broadway actress. Bob entered the theater as a child actor on Broadway in *The American Way*, with Frederic March, and *Watch on the Rhine*, with Paul Lucas.

He began his advertising career as writer/director and senior group producer at the New York City office of the N.W. Ayer Advertising Agency. After that, he managed the audio-visual department of H. G. Peters and Company in Philadelphia (now Production Associates), where he worked on many major accounts. During this period, he won over fourteen awards for his writing and direction of industrial films and programs.

Barron lives in New York's Manhattan, three blocks from where he was born, with his wife (and former pupil), Joyce McCord, and their two daughters, Dana and Allison.

Together, the authors founded and run the Weist-Barron School, one of the largest and best-known schools of acting for television commercials and soap operas in the country.

Introduction

While watching TV commercials you have probably said to yourself, "I could do that!" It looks so easy and natural. But then certain questions come to mind.

Am I a commercial type?

In the early days of TV the young and the beautiful had a corner on the market. But the ad agencies soon learned that the average viewer had difficulty identifying with the glamorous peformer. A typical housewife would remark, "I just can't believe that beautiful model washes her own clothes." Yes, the glamorous gals still sell the hair products, the cosmetics, and the perfumes, the good-looking young men sell the cars and men's grooming products, but the vast majority of products are sold by people who could be your next-door neighbor—people with whom the viewer can identify.

Just look at your TV. Do you see someone about your age, your general appearance? We're sure you will. But even if your looks are out of the ordinary, your very "unusualness" may make you salable. A student who could best be described as "unusual" once entered the Weist-Barron School of Television Commercial Acting in New York. He had very large, deep-set eyes, thick eyebrows, thick glasses, and a large mouth that stretched into an extremely toothy smile. How could such an individual find work on TV? One month after completing his course he had appeared in three commercials. He had no lines to say in any of them. He had been cast because of his unusual look.

How about my voice?

"I don't sound like an announcer." The day has long passed when the advertiser sought the performer with the dulcet, well-rounded tones. You may still hear the "beautiful" voices and not see the performer, but most advertisers do not want the person selling their product to "sound like an announcer." On the other hand, your voice should not be extremely nasal or high and squeaky. Does your voice irritate others? If so, you should get voice training before you attempt commercials. But if you have a good, average voice, speak distinctly, and sound like "that neighbor next door," your speech will be perfectly acceptable.

Has anyone ever said, "You have a great voice on the telephone"? Then maybe you should tackle the voice-over field.

But I have an accent!

Some years ago a man from the Deep South was auditioning for the position of a staff announcer with a major network. He was turned down. Later a friend asked him how he did at the audition. "They're a bunch of damn Yankees and hate Southerners. The excuse they gave was my accent, but I only said 'you all' once."

A heavy regional accent is seldom usable in a national commercial, unless the commercial specifically calls for the accent. It may be usable and even desirable in a local market (if not too heavy) when you are playing a character on camera. If you listen to your local stations (radio and TV) you have no doubt discovered that the voice-over portions of the TV commercials and the radio commercials of local announcers are relatively free of regional accent.

How do you get rid of an accent, or at least tone it down? Let's discuss first the psychological aspects of changing speech. To start off, you have to *want* to change your speech. Some people are afraid that if they change their speech, their friends will think they are putting on airs—that their speech is "affected." On a boat trip once, a well-known voice teacher got well acquainted with a typical New Yorker who had scarcely a trace of a New York City accent, except that he pronounced "world" as "woild," and "oil" as "erl." When questioned about his pronunciation, he replied huffily, "I suppose you think I should say 'world' and 'oil.' " He knew how to say the words correctly but was afraid of being considered "affected" by his friends if he did not use "New Yorkese"!

Remember, *all speech is affected.* We have to copy someone—our parents, our schoolmates, the people in the town or city where we grow up. In France a boy was discovered who had lived with a mother wolf and her cubs until he was about eleven or twelve. He did not talk—but he barked!

The story makes a point. We affect our speech from those around us, and if we want to get rid of, or tone down an accent, we listen to speech that is accent-free and try to copy it—to "affect" it. Record passages of accent-free speech on a cassette—commercials, film narration, anything. Note the length of the passages and leave spaces on the tape so you can copy vocally what you have recorded. It will take time and concentration—changing speech is not easy and will not happen overnight.

If there is a good speech teacher in your area, you can combine your "homework" with a few lessons. The money invested will be well spent.

Make your speech transformation a project. Work on it every day. Don't let your friends kid you about your "affectation." Your "affectation" could mean money in the bank for you someday. So get going.

You've nothing to lose—but your accent.

I have a speech defect

A speech defect obviously presents quite a problem. It is very difficult to remedy by yourself. You should consult a speech therapist and take a course in speech correction. Maybe your problem is sloppy articulation, maybe something more serious. In any event you must often rebuild your entire mechanics of speech. (Even if you never intend to speak professionally, you should nevertheless avail yourself of speech therapy to improve both your business and social relations.)

The possibility of earning money with a speaking part in a commercial or in an industrial film should be a strong motivation for you to take the steps to correct your speech. Of course, there are exceptions, such as the new student at our school who, reading for the first time, displayed a terrible lisp—every "s" came out as a thick "th." Her instructor took her aside after class and quietly told her that if she expected to get speaking roles she would have to do something about her lisp, and he showed her how to correct it. To his utter amazement, when she returned next week, the lisp had entirely disappeared. He congratulated her on overcoming her impediment so quickly. She thanked him, and then said sadly, "But I can't continue with the course." "Why not?" her instructor asked. "Because I have to talk with a lithp," she said. Her perplexed instructor asked, "For heaven's sake, why?" She hung her head. "Becauth my huthband thinkth ith cute."

Let's hope you don't have a lisp, but as indicated earlier in this book, there are areas of employment that do not require you to be speaking: extras in commercials and other film work, even principals in commercials where you are selected because of your type but have no lines. Study the section on pantomime well, because your ability to react to using the product (eating, drinking, etc.) may win you the commercial. Also look into modeling. Many performers find modeling a very lucrative adjunct to their performing career.

Have I the right personality?

Are you an introvert? Are you unfriendly? Do you go around with a glum look on your face, never smiling? Do you avoid looking at people? Do you drop your head and mumble your words when you talk to people? Then commercials are probably not for you. You would have to change your personality completely. It could be done. It has been done, but it's not easy.

On the other hand, are you friendly? Do people like you? Do you enjoy conversing with people? Do you like parties—preferably small ones, where you really get to know people and converse one to one? Were you ever in a play in grammar school, high school, or college? Are you an extrovert? You don't have to be, but sometimes it helps, for then you are less likely to resist trying new speech patterns that may be foreign to your way of speaking. If you have any of the above personality traits, you have good prospects of becoming a successful commercial performer.

But there is one other personality trait you must possess: sincerity. You must have seen commercial performers on the tube whose sincerity you doubted. Perhaps their whole attitude turned you off. Maybe they smiled too much. Hamlet says: " . . . one may smile and smile and be a villain." A smile that is not sincere is worse than no smile at all. Be pleasant, of course; smile when you have something good to relate, and be serious if you are stating a problem. Above all, be involved in what you are saying; then your sincerity will involve your viewers.

How Much Money Can I Make?

A better question would be, "How much money can I expect to make?" In the two largest markets, New York and Los Angeles—Hollywood—yearly earnings can run into the six figures for the top performers—those who have spent years in the business and built solid reputations. We must point out, however, that the average performer makes nowhere near that amount of money. Many just manage to eke out a living, and they often supplement their income with odd jobs unrelated to the commercial or film business. Others find the business a way of supplementing an income from another source. It is the glamor of the business and the lure of making a fortune that draws performers to the two largest commercial centers.

It has been said, and we believe with a great amount of truth, "If you are good, you can make it in a local area. To make it in New York or Los Angeles you must be very, very good." Far be it for us to attempt to discourage the performer of outstanding ability from making the leap to the major centers. We certainly give you the how-to's relating to New York and Los Angeles, but the main thrust of this book is to point out the opportunities in local markets—part- or full-time jobs that may supplement your present income or become your main source of income and give you valuable experience if you ever head for the big time.

Elsewhere in this book you will find the schedule of payments for performers in commercials made under the jurisdiction of the American Federation of Television and Radio Artists (AFTRA) and the Screen Actors Guild (SAG). The schedule will be in effect through the year 1984, when a new contract will be negotiated. In 1985 and thereafter you will have to contact your nearest union office for revised rates of payment. Most of the money—by far the greatest amount—is made in reruns (called "residuals"). By consulting the tables in the current schedule and doing your own arithmetic you will discover that just a single commercial with healthy reruns can net five or ten thousand dollars, or maybe even more. So when you see those commercials being played over and over again on the tube, just say to yourself, "That could be me. And if it were me, I wouldn't be bored, no matter how many times I had to sit through the commercial!"

In cities with no AFTRA or SAG jurisdiction, your rates of payment will vary with the locale; the larger the area, the more you are likely to receive. Sometimes the pay for a day's work will equal union payment, but you may get nothing at all for the reruns. When doing union work you *may* always negotiate for more money than the established scale. When you do nonunion work you generally *must* negotiate your wages. Negotiating for more money is not easy unless you happen to have some clout. Perhaps you are well known in the community, perhaps you have a track record in performing in previous commercials. Maybe you are a model and can insist upon your hourly modeling rate. Unless you can command more money, be content with what is offered. It will almost always be the going rate. Seldom will anyone take advantage of you.

Make certain at the outset that there is agreement as to what you will receive. Some beginners are so anxious to get the work they have no idea of what the payment is until they receive their check.

You might be asked if you would appear just for the experience— let's say on a cable show. Weigh the benefits. You might just be wasting your time. On the other hand, you may get exposure that will help in getting a paying job.

As you have no doubt gleaned from all the above, it is impossible to give you an estimate of the amount of money you can expect to make in commercials and films, because there are so many variables: how often you work; the class of commercials (local or national, program or spot); whether you are classed as a principal or an extra; whether there are reruns, and if so, how many times and in what markets, etc. All we can tell you is that there is money out there. Go get it.

Employment
Opportunities

Commercials

National Commercials

The majority of national commercials are filmed or taped in New York or Hollywood. Since most of the large advertising agencies are located in New York, Hollywood runs a distant second, but producers using the services of Hollywood stars often select Hollywood for their filming. In addition to the proximity of stars and also actors for lesser roles in their commercials, the scenic backgrounds available for exterior shooting may be a factor in determining their filming location.

National commercials are also made in many other cities. The Screen Actors Guild, the union for film actors, has branches in eighteen other large cities, where feature films, industrial films, and national commercials are made: Atlanta; Boston; Chicago; Cleveland; Coral Gables, Fla.; Dallas; Denver; Las Vegas; Lathrup Village, Mich.; Minneapolis; Nashville; Philadelphia; Phoenix; St. Louis; San Diego; San Francisco; Seattle; and Washington, D.C. To work in national commercials in these cities it is necessary to become a union member. When you are chosen to make your first commercial, the production company or advertising agency procures a waiver from the Guild; after the commercial is made you join the union.

There are numerous advantages to becoming a union member. There is an established scale of payments, both for making the commercial and for its replays (residuals). This means that you do not have to negotiate for your payment. If you are a model, however, or someone who can command a higher salary, you can negotiate for overscale payments. The union protects you every step of the way as to working conditions, working hours, and overtime payments. In addition, the union has pension and welfare plans for those who qualify on the basis of yearly earnings.

There is one disadvantage to joining the union: Once you are a member, you may not work in nonunion productions. Of course, this works both ways. Since the union actors living and working in the previously mentioned cities cannot work nonunion, it opens up employment for nonunion members in many local commercials made by production companies who have not signed with the union.

Local Commercials

In every community large enough to have a TV station there is a fertile field of employment in local commercials. Even in the cities that have Guild branches, many local commercials are made. The majority are made nonunion. Performers may appear on film or tape in any of these, or just the performers' voices may be heard giving the sales pitch—doing the voice-over. Radio commercials for local stores and institutions are often made at a local radio station, using the voice of a staff announcer, but to liven up cut-and-dried copy you will often also hear the voices of individuals who purport to be users of the product or service. These are usually local performers.

Now comes the very important first step in seeking employment in local commercials. Watch your TV station (or stations) every hour of your free time. Make a list of all local commercials. Check your local radio station for the same, especially during early-morning and early-evening hours, when you will find the most commercials. If you work during the day, ask friends who watch TV during the day to check for you. Put those youngsters who are glued to the set to work for you.

Now contact your local TV station. Ask for the advertising department and inquire if local talent is being hired. Try to get an interview, which may not be easy; at least ask if you may submit your picture and résumé. Since live commercials often appear on local talk shows, it is always a good idea to ask for an audition. If you have something of a name in your community—if you are president of the PTA or Junior League, for instance—don't be afraid to throw your weight around. Say that your name and face will be recognized and thus give believability to the sales message.

If there is a cable TV outlet in your community, do the same with it. Cable TV is expanding by leaps and bounds, and locally produced shows with local TV messages are offering stiff competition to the regular stations, especially to morning network reruns.

Now search through the yellow pages for the names of all the film production firms in your area. Look under several headings: "Commercials: Radio and Television," "Television Program Producers,"

"Motion Picture Producers and Studios," and other headings that seem relevant, since listings are different in the classified directories for different cities. When you call, ask about commercials *and* any other film work that may require performers.

Other Film Employment

The field of audiovisual communication is growing so rapidly that new areas of employment are continually opening up. Companies desirous of getting the optimum results from their personnel make training films to demonstrate how best to perform various jobs. These films may be shot in the company building or in local film studios, if there are any in the area. Since it would be virtually impossible to contact every large company in your area, again check with local film studios, specifically about training films. The home office of the giant Burger King chain is located in Miami, Florida, and all their industrial films, training films, etc., are done locally and are cast by local agents using nonunion talent. (National spots, however, are done with union talent.)

If there is a large factory where you live, it is more than likely that you'll find they produce a film from time to time demonstrating how their product is made. The film is produced solely as a sales aid, but if it also has an educational or pictorial aspect, it will often be distributed to television stations around the country to be used, free of charge, as a "filler" in time slots that are hard for the station to sell, such as Sunday morning. These films are called industrials. They use the personnel of the plant but often augment their cast with local performers, and almost always a voice-over narrator is hired to describe the action. An out-of-town production company may be doing the production, so check with the factory itself to learn who is in charge of publicity. Then make your call.

Some training films are not motion pictures; instead, still films, or slides, are used, thus cutting costs considerably. Performers may be used both in the still pictures and on the voice track that is synchronized with the slides. Your source of information about slide films is again the production company.

At exhibitions, such as art shows, or large commercial exhibits—the boat show, the automobile show—there will often be a device that plays a series of images over and over again. Pictures are thrown on a small screen, and a narrator's voice is heard describing the products pictured. Once more check local film companies.

The final category where there is a possibility of local employment is the educational film. Colleges, high schools, hospitals, libraries, and museums often make films for classroom instruction or to inform the public of available services. Boy and Girl Scouts, YMCA's, and Police Athletic Leagues may make films to be used on local TV to alert the public to their activity. Hometown charities will band together to make a TV film for a fund-raising campaign. Local summer camps run by charitable organizations often use TV. Check local film companies and the various organizations directly.

By listing all these opportunities for TV and radio commercials and local film productions we do not mean to imply that all are to be found in any given area. It is up to you to ferret out all you can in your hometown and make your own contacts.

Backstage Yearly Directory

Backstage, a New York show biz weekly, publishes a yearly *TV Film and Tape Production Directory,* which should be in the hands of every aspiring commercial or industrial film performer. Among the listings: ad agencies in New York, Chicago, Los Angeles, and San Francisco; production companies in the larger cities—New York; Chicago; Los Angeles; San Diego; San Francisco; Pittsburgh; Philadelphia; Cleveland; Charlotte, N.C.; Minneapolis; Detroit; Baltimore; Washington, D.C.; Denver; New Orleans; Alaska; Hawaii; and Puerto Rico. The states of Arizona, Georgia, Florida, and Texas have separate listings, along with the New England states and Canada. In addition, there are listings for production companies in 135 smaller cities throughout the 50 states. The New York SAG-AFTRA-franchised agents are listed, along with every TV station in the 50 states.

This directory can be purchased at the *Backstage* offices: 330

West 42nd Street, New York, NY 10036 and 5670 Wilshire Boulevard, Hollywood, CA 90036, or it can be ordered by mail from the New York office. The cost is $15.00 plus $3.00 for shipping and handling.

Jingles

Have you sung in a college glee club, or in a church choir? If so, you should be able to read music, and that is a "must" for another radio or TV job—jingle singing. Jingles are those little ditties you often hear in commercials where a single voice or a group of singers sell the product to music. It may be just an introduction to the dramatic copy, it may comprise the whole commercial, or it may be just a tag at the end. For years a soprano sang a soporific song that ended a sleeping pill commercial: "Take Sominex tonight and sleep, sleep, sleep." McDonald's jingle, "You deserve a break today," Burger King's "Have it your way," and "Things go better with Coke" are all examples of catchy tunes that have come to be as well known as Stephen Foster favorites.

The jingles we have mentioned are all "nationals." But what about your local TV commercials or local radio commercials? (Sometimes local stations identify themselves with a jingle.) First, listen as much as you can to your local stations, identify the local spots that are using jingles, then call the station, ask for the advertising manager, and find out what agency made the commercial. Then call the agency to find out who produced the jingle. It is usually a separate production company from the one that produced the rest of the commercial. Call the company that produced the jingle and say you'd like to audition.

Another way to locate jingle producers (here we go again!) is to consult the yellow pages under Recording Studios, for most jingles are made there.

And in New York City you'll find jingle producers listed in the yearly special issue of *Backstage*.

In auditioning for a job singing jingles, the importance of being a "good reader" cannot be overemphasized. No one is going to hum the music for you or play it on the piano when you're doing a jingle. It'll be like *The Lawrence Welk Show,* when Welk says, "Uh one, uh two, uh three" and they're off. You'll start to sing, alone or in a group. You may be singing the melody line or harmony, and you'll be expected to be note-perfect the *first time out!*

Modeling

Probably the most overlooked area for employment in the smaller market is the field of modeling. By "models" we do not mean just the glamor girls with the slim (sometimes *too* slim) figures, nor the Adonis-like men who look like models for the old-time Arrow Collar ads. We mean ordinary men and women who could be "your next-door neighbor," who bring believability to local print ads, or who are photographed to appear in industrial pamphlets for company promotion.

Unless your community is fairly large, there probably will not be a model agency to book your work for you. That means you must do the legwork. Contact your local ad agency or agencies, call local photographers to see if they do print advertising work and for whom, check the advertising departments of local businesses and industries whose ads appear in the newspapers. Department stores use models for ads, and often "live" to display outfits in the various women's wear departments. To show off their clothes to best advantage, you must of course be attractive and have a good figure, but you need not be in your late teens or early twenties. After all, stores do sell to the "mature woman."

If you are going to work consistently as a model, you will have to assemble a photographic portfolio, a collection of pictures showing you in various outfits and poses—head shots and full-length, perhaps a bathing-suit shot if you have a great figure. When you have appeared in a print ad, clip it out and paste it in your portfolio.

Before you invest in your photos, be sure there is modeling work in your area, and then get the opinion of an outsider as to the usability of your type in print ads. Perhaps you can get the advice of someone in the advertising business.

Now for your photos. Shop around for a photographer. See if the photographer has worked on a portfolio for models before. If you like the photographer's work and price, schedule your session, put together your portfolio, and then make the rounds. Your face (or your figure) could be your fortune!

Children in Commercials

Have you a child with an outgoing personality? A child who photographs well? A bright child? A good reader? That child may be able to make more money in commercials than you can, because it is more diffcult to find children who can perform well than it is adults. Perhaps your child is a bit of a showoff—an extrovert. That helps. The shy child, handsome or beautiful as he or she may be, will present a problem when the director is seeking a good performance.

When considering whether your child should seek employment in any branch of show business, the question always arises, "Will the work interrupt his (or her) schooling?" The answer is "yes" if filming that may take several days or even weeks of shooting is involved, as it would be for a feature or industrial film. (Children in Hollywood may have a tutor on the set and can be doing schoolwork when not involved in the actual shooting.)

Commercials, on the other hand, seldom require more than a day of shooting, and the possibility is very slight that the child would make so many commercials during the year that it would seriously interfere with schooling. Most schools let out early enough to permit a child to audition for commercials after school hours. Perhaps the child will miss some favorite TV shows, but winning a few commercials could be a big help toward his or her college education.

If you are a working parent, you may not be able to find the time to accompany your child to auditions and to shooting. If there is someone in your family eighteen years old or over, or someone else whom you can trust, that person may act as your child's guardian both at auditions and at the shooting. One of the provisions of the Screen Actors Guild contract requires that "A parent or guardian must be present at all times while a minor is working, except during schooling. A guardian must be at least eighteen years of age, have the parent's written permission to act as guardian, and show sufficient maturity to be approved by the producer."

There are many other provisions in the Guild contract to ensure the working child's safety and welfare. These provisions apply, of course, only to the cities and areas where the Guild has contracts and jurisdiction. Some companies have purposely moved their production from New York or Hollywood in order not to be bound by Guild agreements and/or the child-labor laws of the particular state. This may bring employment for your child to the area where you live, but then *you* must take the responsibility of seeing to the safety and welfare of your child while he or she is working.

If there is a television acting school in your area, your child could have the opportunity to receive instruction in performing in commercials that will give him or her an edge over the competition at auditions. Although this book is designed to instruct would-be performers of almost any age, it is written primarily for adults. Our Weist-Barron schools schedule a special course for the very young child, and possibly there is a local course in your community.

Employment in New York City

Is a career in one of the major markets your goal? Then it's New York or Hollywood for you. So—you're off to the Big Apple to seek fame and fortune! The lure of the "big bucks" from commercials and other film work brings thousands of hopefuls, young and old, to New York City every year. Yes, there is a bucketful of money waiting for the *very* talented or perhaps just *very* beautiful aspiring performer. Occasionally, but not very often, some people are just lucky, but for the vast majority the road to success is hard. It calls for training, assiduous preparation, dedication, and persistence. If you do not happen to live in New York City or within easy commuting distance, you must think about how you are going to support yourself until you become an established commercial performer. Where will you stay, and how much will it cost? You might start out by living at a

"Y." Your room will be small—just a "hole in the wall"—but it will be clean, and although not cheap, it is probably the least expensive accommodation you can find. Call in advance to determine rates and to make a reservation. Y's also have cafeterias where the food is plain but comparatively low-priced. A Y cafeteria is also a place where you might meet someone who would like to share an apartment with you to save money on rent and food. But be warned: Inexpensive apartments, even very small ones, are hard to find.

Unless you have put aside a fat bankroll, you will have to find a part-time job, and it should give you the opportunity to pursue your career during business hours. Many fledgling performers work as waiters or bartenders. The work is hard, but the tips are good. Are you a good typist? Can you tutor? Would you baby-sit? Part-time work is available in these areas. Consult the Sunday section of *The New York Times* for employment opportunities and for the names of agencies through which you may land a part-time job; also refer to the yellow pages of your phone book.

Sources of TV and Film Work in New York City

Well, you're ensconced in living quarters, you have that part-time job, or you're living off your savings. Now to start your career and get that work you *really* came here to find.

First you will need a *Ross Report,* a small directory published once a month. It gives the names of all the important advertising agencies and their casting directors; film producers and their casting directors; independent casting directors; soap opera directors and casting directors; and other valuable information. It is accurate and is updated every month. It can be purchased at 150 Fifth Avenue; at the office of AFTRA, 1350 Avenue of the Americas (if you are an AFTRA member); at the Drama Bookstore, 723 Seventh Avenue; or at Model Mart, 17 East 48th Street.

Advertising Agencies

There are forty advertising agencies currently listed in the *Ross Report*. These are the primary producers of TV commericals. Some of them maintain offices in Los Angeles as well. Most large agencies retain elaborate casting departments. You can usually tell the size of the agency by the number of casting directors—their names are listed under the agency's name. There are, however, smaller agencies, not listed in the *Ross Report,* that occasionally make commercials. They seldom maintain casting departments, doing their casting through independent casting directors. It is worth a telephone call to find out if they ever see outside talent or will accept photos. Consult your yellow pages.

Independent Casting Directors

Some ad agencies have decided they can save money by eliminating their casting departments and have their casting done by an outside agency. Most of these agencies accept photos and résumés but will see you only if sent by an agent. Some ad agency representatives will attend "showcases" if they feel it is worth their while. Some agencies will view videotape cassettes, listen to voice-over reels, etc. All this information is listed and coded in the *Ross Report.*

New York Television Talent Agents

Talent agents are your most important means of entry into the field of commercials or other show-business employment. Since agents are entitled to 10 percent of your earnings under Screen Actors Guild contracts, it is in their interest to represent the best possible talent. Most, therefore (but not all), accept pictures and résumés. Some represent "signed clients" only. Your chances of being "signed" at the outset are slim, since most of these agents are interested only in representing proven money-makers in the field.

Most agents are busy from morning until night sending talent on audition, so a good, exciting photograph is your best entrée. Remember, however, that every agent maintains a "stable" of various types of actors. For example, six midwestern women; five society women; four character women; eight spokeswomen; five ethnic women; two New York types; five model types, etc. If they have already listed plenty of your type in their stable, they won't respond to your letter, no matter how good your photo may be. But keep trying. There are always agents whose stable lacks strength in some category; if you fit that vacant slot, they will call you in.

Some agents have facilities for playing videotapes, voice-over reels, etc. (The *Ross Report* will indicate this.) A videotape made on a home recorder will evoke little or no interest, but if you have good-quality copies of commercials that you have made for local or regional markets on your tape, submit the tape with a letter explaining where the commercials were telecast and for what products, along with the name of the local advertising agency or production company. Also get copies of any radio commercials you may have done. They can be incorporated in your voice-over tape.

Some agents will attend theatrical "showcases," where you will perform. But their attendance will depend largely upon their interest in you. You must have made an initial personal contact. There are hundreds of showcases produced every year, and an agent cannot be expected to spend all of his or her evenings in the search for talent. For the names of those who will attend selected showcases, again, see the *Ross Report*.

Casting is usually done for New York producers of TV commercials by the ad agency that employs them to make the commercial. But some "creative" and prominent producers insist upon the right to do their own casting, and they have a casting director on the premises. It is worth a phone call to these latter to elicit information. You will find that at least some of them will accept pictures and résumés.

Industrial and business film producers usually do not have a casting director. Nor are they frequently visited by actors. So the few they get to know sometimes reap unexpected work.

There is a yearly guide of industrial producers published by *Backstage* magazine.

Slide Film Producers

Slide films are a less expensive way of producing training or promotional films. Instead of moving pictures, a series of still slides are printed on a film strip, and a sound track is recorded to accompany the pictures. Models are often cast for the pictorial presentation, or actors are sent from the talent agencies. The sound track is recorded by actors who may be cast directly by the producer or by an agent. The more prominent of these companies are signed by AFTRA, pay union scale, and their names may be obtained from the AFTRA office. There are, however, a number of other companies, who operate "out of a briefcase." They maintain a small one-room office where a script is prepared, peddled to a client, and all the other services—photographers, sound studios, etc.—are hired for a single production. These producers are hard to locate. Inquire at a sound studio where you are doing a recording. Ask if they do slide film recording; if they say yes, get the names of the producers. Your pay may or may not be the equivalent of union scale. Of course, if you are a union member you may not work for a nonunion producer, but nonunion slide films could be a source of income for you until you join a union.

Showcases

If you are an actor looking for a part in a major Broadway production or seeking employment in commercials, look into "showcases." A showcase may be a new play by a struggling young playwright, a revival of a classic, or a series of scenes from various plays produced by a group of actors who want to be "seen" in a part they think suitable to them. Agents attend some showcases—the ones in which they have a particular interest. They may have met an actor in an interview who impressed them and whom they would like to see working. If that actor happens not to be *you*, but someone else in the showcase production, the agent will see you too if you're a member of the cast.

Don't expect remuneration from showcases. Sometimes you even have to pay a nominal fee to take part. You may be sharing expenses with other actors for a suitable place to put on the production, but a chance to be seen is worth the investment. In addition to the exposure you will get from a showcase, you are working at your trade—improving yourself as a performer.

Some showcases, either Equity or non-Equity, are listed in *Backstage*, and if a fee is involved, it will say that. How to choose the right showcase? A difficult question. As you are "making the rounds," auditioning, perhaps attending classes, you will meet many others like yourself who are out to make it in the big city. Ask questions. Those who have been around are always ready with advice, and they may have heard of a showcase not listed in *Backstage*.

The Broadway Play

Ah, well, now you have it made as far as exposure is concerned. Most agents make it their business to attend every Broadway play that is produced (if it lasts long enough!), especially if they are given tickets by the actor involved. Now is the time really to get going on your promotion—mailing postcards with your picture and the announcement of the play, phone calls offering tickets. You'll have to pay for the tickets, but it will be a worthwhile investment. Try for at least a few opening-night tickets. Agents will be impressed, and if you are unfortunate enough to be in a short-lived play—enough said! Let's hope it plays for years!

Employment Off-Broadway

Off-Broadway and off-off-Broadway plays are fast becoming very important parts of the New York theater. The good plays are well attended, and those of special merit often make it to Broadway. The cost of producing a Broadway play is so prohibitive that many plays try out off-Broadway, where production costs are much lower. Agents will visit a good off-Broadway play as well as a Broadway play. Casting opportunities are often posted in *Backstage*.

Agents will also attend summer-stock productions if they are not too far from the city. An invitation to attend an out-of-town performance with the added incentive of dinner at a bucolic country inn would be an inducement to many an agent to leave the city to see you. Again, consult *Backstage* for information about summer-stock companies.

We have mentioned *Backstage* several times. It is a weekly newspaper that lists the current castings of theatrical productions not being done in "closed" sessions—both Equity and non-Equity. It is the weekly bible of theatrical performers and can be purchased on the newsstands.

The New York Times

A daily advertising column is published by the *Times*. Sometimes it gives you a lead on new advertising campaigns. The name of the product and the advertising agency will be listed. Many of these campaigns are "after the fact"—that is, the casting and production may already be completed—but sometimes it's worth a try. Contact the ad agency and ask to speak to someone on the account. You might have called in time.

Modeling in New York

Modeling in New York is big business. After all, New York City is the advertising capital of the country, if not of the world. Modeling agencies abound, and if you are lucky enough to be signed with one of them, you won't have to worry where your next meal is coming from. High-fashion models, like those who work through the Ford Agency, earn as much as $250 an hour, and their yearly income can run into six figures. Their work includes posing for print ads in newspapers and magazines, and appearing live in showrooms and fashion shows.

Modeling as a "Door" to Commercials

Once models, male or female, have established themselves, the agencies try to get them work on commercials. The glamor girls smile enticingly, twirl their heads to show what a hair product has done for them, or try to look their sexiest as they whiff a bottle of perfume. The trouble is that many of them, when they open their mouths, do not "speak with the tongues of angels" and haven't the slightest idea how to read lines to make them sound "natural."

The wise models, who want to be heard as well as seen, attend schools, such as our Weist-Barron School, where they can learn commercial techniques. And these are not just the young models. A wise model realizes that she is not going to be able to sell her looks forever. When she is no longer hired to do a cover for *Vogue,* maybe she could work in a commercial, selling a breakfast food loaded with vitamins and minerals.

If you are young, slim, tall (fashion models should be at least five-feet-seven), and gorgeous, you could first become a model and then make it into commercials through the back door.

But don't immediately cut all of your family ties and hop a plane to New York. Plan to come to the city for a few months to try your luck. Get a copy of the *Madison Avenue Handbook* (you can buy it at Model Mart's offices at 17 East 48th Street) and make the rounds.

We mentioned earlier that you will need a portfolio of representative shots for modeling. If you have had one prepared for local modeling work, bring it to New York with you. Although you may want to have another made that has a "New York look," your local portfolio will at least give the agency that you hope will hire you an idea of how you photograph.

Of course, not all models are fashion models. You see all kinds of people in magazines selling all kinds of products—young people, old people—they are all models, and there are agencies for many kinds of models. Is your nose huge? Is your smile too big and toothy? Is your face long and gaunt, or is it as round as a billiard ball? Try Funny Face Brigade, a division of the Sanford Leish Agency. Are you a little chubby? Do you bulge at the seams? Try Plus Models. There are at least seventy-five model agencies or schools listed in the Manhattan yellow pages—many of them specializing. Contacting them all should keep you busy and out of mischief, at least for a while.

Many actors whose goal is the Broadway stage, a running part in a "soap opera," or a well-paying commercial, find modeling a good way to supplement their income. So if you come to New York and don't land that Coca-Cola commercial (which could make you rich!), look into modeling. And remember, you're never too old to model.

Many model agencies are listed in the *Ross Report*. For others, consult the yellow pages. But beware! Some "agencies" will try to sell you a course!

The Agent

Fifi Oscard, of Fifi Oscard Associates, Inc.

An agent provides the actor with the opportunity to work. It is the agent's job to discover what auditions are available, what characters are needed, the product that is being sold, and then to get the actor an appointment to audition for the job. It is the actor's responsibility to "book"—to win—the audition.

For his or her work in procuring the job for the actor, the agent is entitled to ten percent of the gross income earned from that job. This is how an agent makes a living. You can assume, therefore, that an agent is interested in actors who are easy to book.

The stereotypical idea of the agent as loud, overweight, cigar-chewing and money-hungry does not exist in actuality. When you visit an agent's office, you will discover hard-working, earnest men and women who are interested in the development of an actor's career. It may appear difficult to get an interview with an agent, because they do spend most of the time during the day talking on the phone, looking for work for actors they already represent, submitting actors for different jobs and placing calls to the actors. Agents do not have time for actors calling in to introduce themselves, or actors dropping by to try to make appointments. You will find notes on doors at agencies which read "Do Not Enter or Call." This seems harsh, yet there is very little time during the working day for agents to get all the work done that is before them, as it is.

How *do* agents see new people? Wouldn't you imagine they would like to know the new and exciting talent that is available? Of course they would. Agents are always interested in finding talented, professional actors who are willing to work, or "promising" young actors who are being trained. Showcases, Off-Broadway productions, and Broadway shows are perfect ways for you to be seen by an agent. Send a notice of the production to the agents, along with reviews, if there are any. Or, if you are in an acting class that allows agents to review your acting scenes, have the teacher call and invite the agent. A call from a teacher carries more weight than one from you yourself. Have the director who worked with you in school workshops or showcases call the agent to rave about you.

In any case, be sure you are well-trained, your pictures and résumés are professionally prepared, and you have your monologues polished before you meet and audition for an agent. Remember, an agent is interested in representing actors who work. It's that simple. The competition is stiff and gets more so every season. There are no paid understudies in commercials; only one person is booked per role. Therefore, it is your responsibility to be well-trained and professional, to continue studying and practicing your craft. A professional athlete cannot expect to compete to win without daily workouts. As a working actor, you must follow the same rigorous plan.

Signing an Exclusivity Contract

When an agent finds a good actor, he or she will often want exclusive use of the actor's services, and will ask the actor to sign a contract to that effect. In New York, the actor has the option of being represented exclusively by one agent or of "free-lancing" with many agents. The agent will submit the actor with whom he or she has exclusive representation before submitting the free-lancers, thus increasing that actor's chances of being seen.

If the agent assures you that you can make a living through his or her efforts, and you agree, by all means sign and see what happens. If you are starting out, you may prefer to free-lance to ensure enough auditions for yourself to make a living. After all, each agent hears of only a small percentage of the jobs cast in New York in a year.

Don't feel bad if no one tries to sign you. You are generally not approached for an exclusivity contract until you look like a proven winner, or until an agent has a very strong feeling about you and your potential—a feeling which often comes from observation of your work.

In Los Angeles, an agent is a necessity, and representation is done on an exclusivity basis only. You can be represented by only one commercial agent at a time. This relationship is much like a marriage, so choose wisely. Once you have signed with an agent and find it doesn't "feel right," you may ask to be released from your contract and may find another agent. Be warned, however, that casting directors and agents frown on "agency hopping."

Why You Should Know Everyone in an Agent's Office

The aspiring commercial actor probably thinks that because he (or she) has met one person in an agent's office, the agency "knows" him and are keeping their eyes open for someting that suits his type. Generally speaking, nothing could be farther from the truth. "Out of sight, out of mind." You must keep contacting the agency through postcards, phone calls, and personal visits. Nothing can ruin an actor faster than the self-imposed feeling, "Oh, I don't want to bother them. They don't want to see me." Champions make their own breaks! Get out there and (politely) push!

Agencies, especially the larger ones, are often departmentalized. One or two people handle commercials. Another handles soaps. Still another handles theater, and so forth. They do not, like Siamese twins or triplets, all work together on an order. So, while you may know John Bump, his co-worker, Susan Treat, may be looking for someone just like you, and John Bump will probably never hear about it, even though he occupies the desk right next to Susan Treat—unless she asks for his help. The only reason she would do this would probably be if the order were particularly hard to fill.

Try to get the agent you do know to introduce you to the others you don't know. Naturally, each agent will want to appraise your particular qualifications for the kinds of job assignments they handle.

First Steps

Should I Change My Name?

Before making photographs, which can be expensive, give a second thought to your name. Some performers think they will be typed if their name has an ethnic ring. Others change their names because they feel their own names are difficult to say or spell.

This is a difficult topic. If your name is distinctly ethnic and if you are distinctly ethnic, it is probably of no value to change your name.

But many people with the name "Fernandez," or "Spanguelli," or "Pulenski," or "Ginsberg" do not really look ethnic. When, however, you have a "foreign" name, agents and casters expect you to look ethnic when you drop in to see them, despite the fact that your photo did not. This can turn them off before they have seen you, or it may pigeonhole you into a limited supply of work: commercials for spaghetti, enchiladas, or Manischewitz wine!

To find a new name, look into the maiden name of your mother or other relatives and do some "rearranging." Shorten or "Americanize" your real name—or just pick one out of the telephone book or the air. "Bogdoniwicz" could become "Bogden"—a neutral name and one easy to remember. It's a funny thing, but if casters know you're ethnic, they think of you as "ethnic." But if they don't know, they will probably accept you as a generally useful type and you may get more calls. Before changing your name, be sure to check with the unions in whose jurisdiction you hope to work. You may not use a name that is the same of a union member. You may even have to change your own name if it is the same as that of someone already in the union.

Photographs

Right at the outset you will need professional pictures and a résumé. First let's discuss the photos. Before scheduling your sitting with a photographer, be sure of your hair styling and your makeup. For a current hair style, check those you see in the commercials. To be sure that your beauty parlor or hair stylist has an exact idea of the style you want, it is possible to get a fairly good picture by photographing the TV picture. Consult your photo supply house for the lens setting, the exposure, and the type of film you should use. Women will find more styles to choose from during the commercials on daytime soap operas, men during the evening hours. Just ready your camera and snap the picture you want. If you miss the shot, the commercial will likely be repeated on the same show or another show later in the week.

Women should be able to get good advice about their makeup from their beauty parlor. Your makeup, of course, should be street makeup. Stay away from a theatrical look. A man has few worries unless his beard looks very dark even after shaving. In that case he should lighten his beard, using a beard stick that matches his complexion. Hair on the face of men—beards and mustaches—will limit the parts they can play, so a decision must be made: to shave or not to shave. We'll discuss that later.

The importance of a good photograph cannot be overemphasized. Since you may not have the opportunity of a personal interview with an agent or caster, this will be your introduction, your way of saying, "Hi, here I am." When a call is put out to you for an audition, you will be expected to show up looking exactly like the picture you have submitted.

Now is the time, before you spend money on your pictures, to decide what type you want to be: a glamor girl or a housewife; a "hard hat" or a businessman. Make your decision with the advice of friends, for we cannot always judge ourselves objectively. Of course, there can be a number of variations within your type. For example, a "professional" could be a doctor, a lawyer, a businessperson, a professor, a scientist, etc.

When the day of your photographic sitting arrives, think of how you should dress, how you should do your hair, and what, if any, makeup you should wear.

Here are a few general suggestions to show you what we mean:

Young glamor girl (the type to advertise hair products, cosmetics, perfumes, etc.): Hair stylish, soft, and full. Glamor makeup, but not too heavy. Full lips, but not too red.

Out-of-doors All-American girl: Solid-color, no-print man's shirt, open at collar. No jewelry.

Sexier (if you want to go this route): Shirtwaist cut lower. (But, careful! Don't be too obvious!) Earrings not large and not pendants. A simple necklace.

Housewife (feeding youngsters, washing clothes, diapering babies, etc.): Hair-do in a current style, but not fluffy, and not in ringlets. Makeup that appears like no makeup. (Careful of the lipstick. Don't make the mouth too sexy.) Shirtwaist dress, open at the collar. No jewelry, not even small earrings.

Young businessman or professional man (car salesman, computer salesman, proprietary-drug salesman, architect, banker): Shirt, tie and jacket (plain without stripes and not plaid). No pattern in tie and shirt, or at most a very conservative pattern. Hair in modern style, not too long (long hair is out!), neatly combed. Beard stick, if after a shave beard looks too dark.

Out-of-doors young man (young father cooking on an outside grill, or selling sports products, men's toiletries, etc.): Open shirt, no jacket or tie, hair well groomed but loose, not overcombed. Beard stick if needed.

And so it goes. You get the idea. If you are more mature, be sure you look it in makeup and dress. You may wear glasses or not. Most agents want to see you without glasses in your picture, although it is a good idea to have several shots taken with glasses at the time of the sitting. Then have the picture made up and submit it if you think the character you are called for might be wearing glasses. Also some people who wear glasses all the time, when photographed without them, look in their picture as if they *need* glasses.

If you're not sure of your type, go with a conventional photo—not too informal nor too dressy or décolleté.

Now you are ready for your sitting. Get plenty of sleep the night before. There's no point overdoing the bags and wrinkles!

The Sitting

Presumably you have selected your photographer after inspecting the work of a number of different photographers—and we mean *professional* photographers.

Don't have a friend do the job for you unless that person is in the business of making head shots. No matter how good a photographer is, his or her work will usually not compare favorably with those who make a daily business of doing only head shots. Then, too, a friend may shoot what he or she wants to shoot, not what you want. And since it is done for free, you may wait a long time to get the results in final form. So use a "head-shot professional." Your money will be well spent. Remember, the sitting and your prints are only part of your expense. From your original print or prints, copies have to be made. Why spend good money on the copies if the original photograph is not a professional picture?

In preparing for a photograph, be aware of these factors:

Makeup (women): Don't appear to be wearing makeup. Some women line their eyes, use excessive mascara and eyeshadow or false eyelashes stuck together like the prongs on the Statue of Liberty's head. Makeup? Sure, but subtly achieved.

Makeup (men): Repress beards with a pan stick, or you will find yourself with seventy-two dirty-looking proofs.

Hair (women): Hairdo in a simple, classic style. When bangs are worn, they are too long if they touch the eyebrows. Hair ends should just touch the shoulders and bounce off. Modern hair styles (crimpled hair, corn rows), while attractive socially, are not considered proper for TV commercial photos.

Hair (men): Hair can be in the modern style, but too long is out.

Expression: A warm, friendly smile. Look straight into the lens and smile—not a half smile, not a frantic smile, just a warm, friendly smile. Don't touch your face, and don't "cock" your head.

Silly poses or fancy shots: The only thing most agents seem to want for commercials is a simple, warm, friendly head shot. Shots with hair blowing in the wind, back-lit shots, and contrasty, dramatic shots are, in their view, a waste of your time and the photographer's—unless, of course, specifically requested for theatrical (as opposed to TV) use.

Black people: Agents tell us that they prefer a "modified" Afro, not too high, not too low. If you don't like this idea, forget it. But that's what the agents say.

Although white subjects with moustaches are generally not accepted for commercials, black males with moustaches seem to dominate TV at this writing.

Glasses: Watch TV and you'll see that glasses are in vogue these days. A lot of young character men seem to do well wearing them. For that reason, we suggest that you buy a pair of frames (without lenses) and have some shots taken with them on—sometimes with a bow tie, as well. Plain, round, ugly black frames seem to be preferred.

Character people: We advise character people to have a simple head shot *and* a composite photograph featuring the head shot plus a series of character shots. However, the character shots should be in different costumes; in many photos, the subject never seems to change costume. Result? The shots look too much alike because the clothes are the same. In the character shots, the clothing may be patterned, and any other type of costume germane to the character may be used.

The following instructions for taking a professional picture for commercial work are pretty standard throughout the industry. We suggest that you show them to your photographer, either from this book or by copying them. You'll not be considered presumptuous; you'll be considered a pro who knows what you want.

Background: Limbo. No walls or other "set." Do not photograph out-of-doors; the background will be distracting.

Lighting: No lights that will produce harsh highlights. Reflected light is best, with needed fill.

Expression: Look straight into the lens. If, in smiling, your gums show, let them show—they're going to show at the interview this photo is supposed to get them.

Angles: The straight-on angle is preferred. But if the subject has a round face or a wide jaw, turn the face slightly off-lens into a semi-three-quarter, to minimize the width of the jawline. Still look directly into the lens.

Cropping the photo: Most agents and casting executives feel that the finished photo should be cropped just below the point of the collar. This sometimes causes a problem with women, parts of whose hair is "lost" on the sides because of the proportions of an eight-by-ten photo. Keep this in mind, but be sure the head is large in your negative.

Retouching: Some photographers forget to remove the reflections from their lights from the subject's eyes. Be sure this is done. If a small space (very dark and small) shows between two central teeth, the photographer should spot it out. But retouching should be minimal. The aim is to enhance your appearance without changing it. An existing mole should remain, but it could be slightly mini-mized. We are talking about a spotting brush, not expensive nega-tive retouching.

Your Contact Prints

The first thing you will get back from the photographer is a sheet or sheets of contact prints. These are small prints, which should be examined with a magnifying glass. Don't make the selection by yourself. Get a consensus. It is hard to be objective about yourself.

Although a little light retouching may be done, do not order so much retouching that the picture no longer looks like you. It will render your picture worthless. For example, if you are sent on a session where they are casting for women in the twenty-two to twenty-five age bracket, and you are forty-five but have doctored up your picture to make you look twenty-five, when they see you as you are, they are obviously not going to let you audition. And because your picture makes you look 25, you will not be called when they are auditioning for forty-five-year-olds. So you lose out both ways.

Just such a situation arose at a prominent ad agency. The audition was for women in their midtwenties. A picture was selected of a woman we'll call Jane Damon, who looked to be about twenty-five from her picture. When Ms. Damon arrived she looked her age, forty-five, despite the heavy makeup designed to cover up the lines, bags, and wrinkles. The casting woman took one look at her and said, "There must be some mistake. The call was for your daughter." Ms. Damon smiled sweetly and said, "Oh, you see, I am that daughter." End of story—end of audition.

You have made your selection from the contact prints. Usually you are allowed more than one selection—maybe two or three. These will be made up into eight-by-ten enlargements so that you will get a better idea of the picture. Sometimes the photographer will supply you with an eleven-by-fourteen matte print.

Again with the help of friends, make your final selection. It is a good idea to make a second selection that you can have made into picture postcards, which you will be mailing later as reminders. Perhaps you will want a photo with glasses as an alternate picture.

Now check your classified directory for Photocopying and make calls to get price comparisons. You'll need about a hundred glossy copies to start with—maybe fewer in a smaller community. You have made your list of the people to whom you wish to send photos. Get a few more than you think you'll need. Here are a few instructions to be observed in the copying:

- The most modern style is to have no borders on your photo.
- Don't print your photo on paper. Paper photos mean you're a model, and in the eyes of TV commercial agents and casting directors, models usually cannot act. So use glossy photos for TV, even though you may have a paper composite for modeling.
- Put your name on the front of the photo.
- If you're a character person, you should have both a simple, friendly head shot and a composite (if you can afford both). But don't have an old-fashioned one, two, three, four composite. Use a little imagination and art direction on the preparation of the composite—perhaps one large photo of yourself (a straight pose), surrounded by some smaller character poses in an "L" shape.

A Final Reminder

Remember: The most important ingredient in your head shot is that it be a "living" picture—that it has a feeling of liveliness. After all, agents get twenty-five to fifty photos a day. Your photo is your calling card, and if you want to be called in, it must attract attention!

For Men Only

"To shave or not to shave?" This presents a dilemma. We are referring, of course, to beards and moustaches. Some men look great with hair on their face, others look slovenly, but if a beard or moustache, or both, are part of your "look," you will naturally feel a reluctance to return to a bare face. You will soon discover from watching the tube that whites with beards and moustaches are very rare in commercials. So to increase your chances of employment, get out your razor, lather your face, take a deep breath—and shave.

Later you may have to tell your girlfriend to dry her tears when she sees you with that naked look. (She thought you looked so handsome and masculine with your beard!) You can console her by saying, "Honey, now maybe I'll get on a commercial and we can take that trip to Bermuda we've always dreamed about."

We can report here an incident that occurred when a well-known actor with a moustache auditioned for a pharmaceutical commercial that would have netted him around ten thousand dollars with all the reruns. He didn't get it. Quite some time later he met the auditioner at a bar. In the course of their conversation the auditioner said, "By the way, the client liked your audition very much. He would have hired you, but he couldn't take you with the moustache." Sadly the actor said, "Why didn't you tell me? I would have shaved off my moustache. I can grow one back much quicker than I can make ten thousand dollars!"

Children's Photos

If you have budding performers in your home, you might want to see what interest in them you can engender when you make the rounds by showing off your home snapshots. Once you have determined that your children might have an opportunity to be employed in commercials, they also will need professional pictures. As much care must be taken with their photographic session as was taken with yours. Be sure their pictures make them look "as bright as a button." A solemn photo of a beautiful child is not going to evoke nearly as much interest as one of a freckle-faced youngster with a grin of devilment in his or her eyes.

Résumés

You have received your glossy photo prints from the copier. The next step is to prepare a résumé.

In the days of radio (that's when ears were glued to a loudspeaker instead of eyes glued to a tube), there was an actor well known for his performances on radio as well as the Broadway stage. Well known, except to a young radio casting director who had reached his exalted position through three months of hard work and the help of a father who happened to be president of the company. He said to the actor, Ed Jerome, "Tell me. What have you done?" After a long look at the upstart, Ed queried, "What have I done? What have I done about what?"

Yes, they'll want to know what you've done, and that's where the résumé comes in. It's really a brief bio that tells what you have done as a performer, prepared in a form that has become standard in the industry. They'll want to know your age. Put down how old you really look. As we have mentioned earlier, it does no good to lie about your age, telling them you are a lot younger than you are, and then showing up looking your actual age. Some actors get around giving their exact age by indicating an "age range." That is not cheating if with makeup, etc., you actually can look either younger or older than you are. (We've noticed in looking over a number of résumés of the women that the top of the age range is their actual age.) Include your union affiliation or affiliations if you have any.

Now comes the question put to Ed Jerome, "What have you done?" In a panic you say, "What have I done? Why, I haven't done anything!" Calm down a moment and think. What about that high school play you were in when you were living in Doylestown? Maybe it would not be stretching it too much to say the play was put on by the Doylestown Players. Well, they *were* Doylestown players—you just capitalized the letter "P."

Then there were college plays. Put them down, maybe naming the college players after the town in which the school was located. Later you may have been in a church play, a local theater group. List everything you can think of and the parts you have played. Be sure you don't lie about the play you were in. You might be asked questions you wouldn't be able to answer. Some actors, if they have not been in any plays, will list representative roles they might well have played. Well, we don't exactly say "no" to this procedure. The trouble is that it is used so much on résumés that it begins to stick out as an indication of not having actually participated in the play and the role mentioned. On the other hand, it's better than nothing.

Have you appeared on any local TV shows? What about radio? Put down any experience you have had which will indicate that you are a serious performer.

Let's say you have had some soap opera experience in New York, but you've only been employed as an extra. If you just list the soap opera, your auditioner is not going to be impressed. It will be obvious at once that you were just an extra. Give your extra a name. After all, the character you were playing must have had a name. So you might list, for instance, *"Search for Tomorrow*—part of Eric Boles." You are not lying—you're just embellishing a bit.

As you can see, we're advising you to "dress up" what you have actually done a little bit. The person interviewing you will undoubtedly have a pretty good knowledge of show business, so don't tell an out-and-out lie. To be caught in a lie could be very damaging to the impression you are trying to make.

Of course, list any industrial or educational films you may have done. List anything you can think of that will show you have had experience appearing before the public —if you've done a lot of public speaking, for instance—and are not just a neophyte.

At the bottom of your résumé list your special skills.

Special Skills and Physical Features

Do you ski (snow or water)? Do you play tennis, roller skate, ride horseback sidesaddle, or scuba? Be sure to list any special skills on your résumé. Your recreational sport may be the deciding factor in your winning a commercial. You see, agents and agency casting directors *do* look at pictures and résumés, especially if the call is for some unusual skill. Some casters maintain a separate file listing skills and the actors having them who can be called if needed.

A New York model we know, then residing in Florida, heard by the grapevine that a commercial was being cast that required a beautiful girl with a divine figure to be photographed scuba diving. Our model friend had all the requirements—except one. She didn't know the first thing about scuba diving. Not to let a little detail like that stop her, she called a friend who had many hours of underwater experience, and over the phone she found out the basics she would need to know for the audition. She showed up for the audition, was asked if she could scuba, answered "yes," and was fitted out with a mask, regulator, and a bottle of air. The dive was made in a huge glass tank and she was photographed undulating as gracefully as if she had been diving all her life. She won the audition, then the next day began a course in scuba diving, which she completed before the commercial was filmed—in the ocean.

Now, we are not suggesting the preceding example as a general procedure. You might get in serious trouble. And if a commercial requires you to dive into a five-foot tank of water from a height of one hundred feet, it would be a good idea to practice once or twice before applying for the job. Our story does demonstrate, however, that a little initiative, now and then, can pay off.

Are you very short or very tall? What you consider a handicap could turn out to be a plus. A memorable commercial for an airline shows a towering famous basketball player taking his seat. Then there enters another famous basketball player who is even taller, to the dismay of the first man. Of course, they were cast because they were both well-known stars. But they were used in the commercial because of all the well-known players, they were the tallest.

Are your teeth your own? Don't laugh—we're serious. If you have a beautiful set of teeth that God gave you, put that on your résumé. The teeth must be perfectly even, glistening white, and you must have a radiant smile to go with them. They cannot be caps, because caps photograph as caps. With a set of beautiful teeth and a toothpaste commercial playing all over the country, you could be displaying that smile all the way to the bank.

You say God didn't give you your beautiful teeth, a dentist did? You might make even more money doing denture products. Because of "truth in advertising" required by the networks, the makers of denture products many times require that you have at least a removable denture. It need not be a complete set of false teeth, but it must be on a bridge that can be taken out. Some time ago, at our school in New York, an actor in his thirties actually had a perfectly good tooth removed and mounted on a bridge so he could do denture commercials! We don't advise that you go to extremes, but don't be ashamed to list dentures on your résumé. Then maybe the next time you bite into corn on the cob, it will be with a battery of lights glaring at you and a camera rolling a few feet away.

Beautiful hair could win you a commercial. Be sure your photograph makes your hair look gorgeous. How about your hands? Are they long, slim, and lovely? Then put that down on your résumé. You could be called to do a hand modeling job. Do people admire your legs instead of your face? Don't despair. You could end up relishing a gourmet dinner with champagne and caviar at a fancy restaurant to celebrate the money you made rolling that sheer hose up your beautiful lower limbs.

And so it goes. Space does not permit the listing of all the casting possibilities to be found in special skills and physical features. But be sure you list yours on your résumé.

Sample Résumé

Actress-Singer-Dancer

Mata J. Hari   AFTRA

Service Phone: (914) 708-9987

Height: 5'8"

Weight: 118 lbs.

Eyes: brown

Hair: brown

Age range: 27–32

Social Security No.: 249-49-0092

Theatrical Experience

Community theater:
(Bennington Playhouse—Bennington, Vt.)   1971-72
Carousel. . . . . Carrie
P.S., Your Cat Is Dead . . . . Kate
Mousetrap . . . . Molly
(Top o' the Barrel—Madison, Conn.)   1973
Come Blow Your Horn . . . . Connie

Television:
TV and radio commercials list upon request

Industrials:
Chic with Schick—Chicago Housewares Show, for Schick, Inc.
Toshiba's ENG Cameras—NAB Convention, Las Vegas, for Toshiba International
Starr's presentation—Pitney-Bowes, Inc.

Spokeswoman:
Schick, Inc.
Toshiba, International

Shake 'n' Bake, General Foods
Pitney-Bowes, Inc.
Aetna Life and Casualty Company

Trade shows:
Including housewares shows, premium shows, auto shows, sporting goods, ski shows, jewelry shows, etc.

Specialties:
Singing, dancing, guitar, fluent German and French, tennis, snow- and water-skiing, diving, sailing, canoeing, horseback (English and Western), ice-skating, bicycling. Licensed driver, can drive tractor and snowmobile. Can diaper babies, do crewel embroidery, *strong* PR background, arts (principal founder, Connecticut Ballet Company), civic, industrial, consumer. (Diversified exposure enables me to address a broad range of target markets.)

Training:
Weist-Barron School, N.Y.C.; Charles Reilly, N.Y.C.

Sample Résumé

Jane J. Waspberg
Actress

Height:	5'8"
Weight:	127 lbs.
Eyes:	brown
Hair:	brown
Age range:	22–26
Service phone:	(516) 780-1188
Social Security No.:	053-12-5621
SAG	AFTRA
AGVA	Equity

Theatrical Experience

Broadway:
The American Way—Fredric March's granddaughter
The Watch on the Rhine—Paul Lucas's daughter

Stock:
(The Agonquit Players, South Maine)   1970–71
The Tender Years—Snicker
Over the Transom—reporter
(Barclay Theater—Kevin, Conn.)   1969–70
Mother Knew—Roger Ames's secretary
Outward Bound—clergyman's sister

Off-Broadway:
  Decrepit Theater—*Fifth*—Jackie
  Finlay Street Players—*Come On*—young wife

Dinner Theater:
  The Gourmet Players (Pittsburgh Dining Center)—*Blithe Spirit*—maid

Radio and TV:
  Let's Pretend—CBS Radio, N.Y.C.
  Search for Tomorrow—CBS-TV, N.Y.C.

Films:
On the Waterfront—Brando's cousin—MGM
Crummy Mack—young prostitute—Paramount

Industrial shows and films:
  Wings over Europe, TWA industrial, Parkas Productions, N.Y.C.
  Two on a Holiday, Esso, H.G. Peters & Company, Philadelphia
  Buick Auto Show—Coliseum, N.Y.C.

Here you have a choice: You can say "TV commercial list on request," or "TV commercials for various New York and (largest town near your home) advertising agencies. If you have no list, don't say you do. Never name the products. You can, however, name the ad agencies, production companies, or the TV or radio station call letters.

Special skills:
  Driver (shift and automatic), acrobatics, water- and snow-ski, guitar, type, weld, sail, ride a horse, roller- and ice-skate, speak fluent French and Spanish.

Training:
  Herbert Berghof Studios, New York; Goodman Theater, Chicago; Weist-Barron, New York

Sample Résumé

Joni Engel
(212) 869-4645

Height:	5'6"
Weight:	118
Hair:	Chestnut
Eyes:	Blue
Voice:	Alto/mezzo soprano
Dress Size:	5

Regional

Sandollar Players Dinner Theater   Pensacola, Florida

Luv...Ellen

Beyond the Fringe...................................Dudley

Jewel Box Theatre   Oklahoma City, Oklahoma

Coupla White Chicks...........................Hannah Mae

Actors Company Theatre   Oklahoma City, Oklahoma

Charlie's Aunt..Amy

Steadfast Tin Soldier ....Raggedy Ann

Voices..Player 3

Representative Roles Played

Musical

Kiss Me Kate ....Bianca

Oliver..Bet

The Mikado ....Peep-Bo

Drama

The Sandcastle ....Joan

The Recluse ....The Recluse

Comedy

Vanities..Joann

It's Called the Sugar Plum ....Joanna

Dirty Linen ....Mrs. Ebury

Classical

Hamlet...Ophelia

Waltz of the Toreadors ....Eugenie

Way of the World ....Foible

Films

Xerox Training Film (Industrial) ....Student

Four Comedy Shorts (Cable TV) ....Leads

Student Films for Oklahoma University ....Various

Training

Acting.............James Slaughter, Alan Langdon, Hilary Lidell

Dance & Movement ....Miqael Terekhov, Anne Cowan

Dialects..........British, Cockney, Mid-western, Southern, Irish

Skills

All sports, roller skating, water skiing, horse rider/trainer, dance instructor (Disco & Western), guitar, bartender, mime, seamstress

Mailing and Making the Rounds

Have your résumés duplicated at a printer's, or put on the back of your photo by the photocopier. The résumé must be the same size as the photo and attached to or printed on the back of the photo.

Now you will need photo mailers, which can be obtained at any stationery shop. Mail a photo with your résumé to every prospect you have lined up from the yellow pages. The mailer should be addressed to the casting director. Include a note saying you would appreciate an interview or an audition. If you have a friend or some personal contact at the company, mail a separate picture and a note saying you have sent a picture to the casting director and you would appreciate their putting in a good word for you.

It is not likely that you will get an immediate response to your mailing. Indeed, you may never get a response, so don't count the hours waiting for a reply. Casting directors do, however, consult their photo files when looking for a specific type, and that is when you may receive a call for an audition or interview.

You must make arrangements for your phone to be answered every minute of the working day, either in person by someone in your family, or by an answering machine or service. A missed call can mean a missed job.

Although it is good form to mail a photo prior to making a personal contact, some performers attempt to make personal contact before mailing their pictures. If you don't have an "in," you may get no further than the outer office, but you can leave your picture and résumé and perhaps elicit some useful information. Is it possible to arrange an appointment? If so, your legwork may pay off. All you have to lose is shoe leather.

The Interview

When you are called for an interview, dress neatly and in good taste. Avoid anything ostentatious that would look as though you are trying to show off. Take along your picture and résumé even though they may have been left previously. Arrange to arrive about ten minutes ahead of time—not too early, it might make you appear overanxious (which you might well be!). When you are ushered in for the interview, be cordial but not "gushy." If you have greetings from a mutual friend, state them briefly and do not elaborate unless your interviewer seeks more information.

You will probably be asked to be seated. Sit erect. Do not slump in your chair. It is OK to cross your legs if it is your habit and you feel comfortable doing so. You must always look and act at ease and confident. Answer all questions concisely but pleasantly. Don't go on and on about any topic of conversation unless you are asked to do so.

You may, however, be asked to "tell something about yourself," so be prepared, or your interview will get off to a bad start.

Here is a sample of an interview between a Mr. Whitney, the advertising executive, and a Mrs. Ross:

Whitney: Mrs. Ross, I'd like to know a little about you. Tell me about yourself.

Ross: Oh, well, now, there really isn't much to tell. Let me see. Well, I'm married and have two children and my husband is a salesman and I live in Farmingdale—we moved there from Jonesport.

Who cares? Not Mr. Whitney, whose time is valuable and who wants to hear more pertinent information.

Now, Mrs. Ross could have said (if it were true, and you must never give false information), "I went to high school in Jonesport and I was in about every play they put on. I graduated from Ohio University in Athens. Some people confuse it with Ohio State (this is thrown in to sound a little chatty. It shouldn't be all cut-and-dried). My major was speech. I was on the debating team and I was in as many plays as I could work into my schedule. I've tried to keep up with acting here in Farmingdale, in the Midtown Players Group. I am married and I have two children. By the way, I brought their pictures, in case you might some time have a call for youngsters. At any rate, next to my family, acting is my first love, and I'm here because I'd like to get into a television commercial."

There it is. Concise, pertinent information. It will impress your interviewer, but be prepared in advance with what you intend to say.

You may be asked to read, so be sure you take a clipboard with you. It makes it easier to take notes, and most important of all, it gives you a stiff backing for any script you may be asked to read. Without a support, a single sheet of paper can bend as you read, and disrupt your concentration. When reading, hold the board high enough so you do not have to drop your head to see the script. Dropping the head momentarily cuts off your communication with the person for whom you are reading.

When you are asked to read copy, take the time to study it. You will not be expected to read it "cold." If there is a choice of copy, choose the one best suited to you. When you finally read out loud, employ the speak-read method outlined later in this book. If you make a mistake, don't apologize and make excuses when you have finished reading. You are not expected to be word-perfect and letter-perfect in a first run-through. If you are given direction and asked to read again, be sure you thoroughly understand the direction before you re-read. In their eagerness, performers often plunge ahead with the second reading because they don't want to appear dense by asking for a repetition of a direction that they have not completely understood.

It is always a good idea to stand up when you read, so ask, "Do you mind if I stand?" Psychologically, standing firmly on your two feet gives you a stronger position. It immediately increases your authority. You yourself will feel more in command than if you were seated opposite the person to whom you are reading. Furthermore, the diaphragm is more efficient when you are erect—breathing and control of breath are at their maximum.

Look directly into the eyes of your listener, not just out into space. If more than one other person is present, divide your "looking" time between or among them, but don't hop back and forth, reading just a few words to one person and then switching to another. A good rule is not to change your attention until you have completed a sentence.

If there is room, shift your position and take a step toward the person you are addressing. You may be surprised at the feeling of command such a move will give you—and it will make an impression on your listener. This step, combined with your eye contact, gives added emphasis to the copy you are reading.

When the interview has been concluded, say your thanks and leave. Take a tip from Lady Macbeth, who said, "Stand not upon the order of your going, but go at once." Don't dawdle. Don't take up the time of your interviewer with idle conversation. Remember, Shakespeare has Polonius say, after boring Hamlet with his wordiness, "My honourable lord, I will most humbly take my leave of you," to which Hamlet replies, "You cannot, sir, take from me anything that I will more willingly part withal." So don't be a Polonius. Say your thanks, good-byes, and leave.

If you have a nine-to-five job, scheduling interviews and auditions will be difficult. Sometimes you can arrange the appointment so it falls within your lunch hour. A better way to take time off is to arrange with your employer to take no lunch hour on the day of your interview so you can be free at the time of your appointment. Another solution is to get an agreement to work overtime for the time you were away from work. Save up vacation days and sick-leave days for the times when you have to do the actual recording of the commercial.

If you are a stay-at-home mother with a child who is old enough to go with you and is well behaved, take him or her along. Who knows? It might lead to a job for the child. Naturally, you don't want your child bursting in on your interview crying, "Mommy!" or "Daddy!" but if you can convince your youngster to sit quietly in the reception room and wait for you, it may be a good introduction to surroundings that he or she may encounter later when starting an acting career.

Follow-up

Phone-call follow-ups are in order, but they should be very infrequent. Your interviewer does not have the time to converse with all the performers who have been auditioned. If you are well acquainted with the person who auditioned you, that's a different story—but still, don't make a nuisance of yourself.

The best method to remind your interviewer that you are still available and would like to work is to send a picture postcard of yourself with a brief note. The first card could be a "thank you" note. Subsequent follow-up cards might contain information about your activities. "I'm appearing with the South Shore Players in *Run for the Money*. It's playing on [give the dates]. It's a fun show. Hope you can make it." Now, the chances are that your interviewer is not going to dash out and buy tickets, but at least it shows that you are doing something. Even if you haven't anything interesting to report, a card now and then, just to say "Hello," is in order. So is a holiday card at Christmas, Easter, etc. How frequently should you mail a reminder? Once a month should be enough.

Most of the photographic reproduction houses will also make your postcards. Some performers use their standard photo on the card; others prefer a picture with a different pose. Be sure that the picture on the card is current and was taken at the same time that your standard photo was made. After all, you don't want the recipient of your card to think that your photo and your card represent two different people.

When you have new photos made you have an excuse to send around a second picture with a note. Or, to save money, just send your postcard with the new picture, saying, "Here's my new look!"

What Casting Directors Look For

Angela Brogna Montalbano

(Angela Montalbano is head of casting at William Esty Advertising Company, Inc., a major advertising agency)

There are many facets to a performer, but I will try to express what seem to me to be the fundamentals I seek when interviewing and casting an actor.

A sense of presence and a positive outlook (or the lack of them) are the first things the casting director notices. They are essential to project the confidence and personality necessary for a better perspective on the performer's ability to deal with an unfamiliar situation.

Awareness of one's self, I think, should be near the top of the list. It helps to bring a fullness to a performance.

I look for an indication that the actor has the ability to understand what it is that we are trying to communicate when giving a direction in order to express the concept of the ad. After a performer has auditioned, and we show the tapes to the producer and director, we will often hear "Now, that performer looks as though he [or she] understands what we're trying to get across!"

I look for a willingness to cooperate, not only in order to give a good performance but to make our job easier and more effective.

Of course, a strong résumé also helps.

We're in a business, and we're looking for people who not only understand the creative aspect, but the business one as well. It's so important to be able to present yourself with confidence, a smile on your face, and an eagerness that says, "Let's get the job done!" Actors in commercials are spokespersons, salespeople, selling first themselves and then the product. Those who do both of these things well get the jobs. Ultimately, the client buys the actor's personality and his or her ability to project the technique that guarantees an outstanding performance.

I look for professionalism. Professionals accept the responsibility of their craft, knowing how to tap that fine instrument within, which, if tuned and refined, can bring forth a great performance. Commercials may seem like the bottom of the barrel, not worth wasting time on, but they afford the actor an opportunity to work in a lucrative field while waiting for that big break in the other world of creative expression, film.

In retrospect, I look for a positive attitude, a high energy level that indicates a worker—someone eager to produce. That's what sells! I look for courtesy, respect, good manners, a knowledge and understanding of protocol. I look for cooperation, dedication, awareness of the craft, personality and charisma—that something special that jumps out at you and says "This person has got it!"

It's all subjective. One can only hope that the idea being conveyed will be like a fine thread that draws all of us to a unanimous understanding of what we need in a performer. Because it is the performer who provides the image that others will emulate once his or her talents have been recognized by the public.

How an Ad's Characters are Conceived

Where do the casting directors get their idea of the type they want in the first place?

The larger agencies have a "Plans Department" or "Marketing Department," which researches and studies the client's problem. (Why isn't the product selling as it used to? How can we sell our soft drink to the geriatric market?)

They come up with a master plan explaining how they expect to

solve the problem. The plan includes the ad themes they will use—
"it has to taste bad to be good," for example. Then the copy people
write the commercial after the plan is approved. But they must write
it to conform to the conclusions of the approved plan. They work
with the art director, and together they come up with the ads. They
do this in the form of a storyboard—a giant-size "comic strip" that
shows in pictures, scene for scene, what will happen in the commercial. The dialogue that will be spoken or narrated during the action is
shown beneath each frame.

The commercial is then sent to the Legal Department for clear-
ances; once that is done, the commercial is set and cannot be
changed.

The rough drawings on the storyboard are then redrawn by an
outside artist, who draws the characters according to his or her idea
of them. Then, if the client approves, the boards are shown to the
Casting Department, and they get their notion of the characters
from that. It doesn't matter that the artist who comes up with the
final version of the characters doesn't even work for the agency. If
this artist drew a blond woman who looks twenty-seven years old,
with her hair parted in the middle, and a kid with ears that stick out
and freckles, the casting department immediately begins to look for
a twenty-seven-year-old blonde with her hair parted in the middle
and a kid whose ears stick out and who has freckles. There are
instances, however, when an agent will send the wrong type and for
some reason that actor will revise the casting director's idea of what
type would really be best—and the "wrong" type gets the part.

An agency was once casting for a rather delicate young man to
contrast with a huge, overbearing mother. They asked an agent to
send over a man we'll call John Meyer. Now, it just so happened that
they called the wrong agency. There was a John Meyer there, too,
but he was a big, strong hulk of a man—a real "hard hat" type. He
showed up at the audition along with a dozen or so slight, somewhat
prissy young men. What did the agency do? They were so amused
by the incident they changed the whole concept of the commercial.
They cast the hard hat and then changed the mother to a wee
eighty-five-pound woman.

The motto must be: Go to any audition you are sent to, even if you
turn out not to be the type. What can you lose? You might just get
lucky.

Auditions on Camera

The Preparation

One of the things the commercial "pros" consider a must is determining before they go to an audition what the character they will be asked to portray is like and what the character is doing. Casting directors have very little imagination—or if they do have any, they prefer not to use it. At an audition they usually like to find someone who looks exactly like what they have in mind for the part they are casting.

If you are sent to an audition by an agent or agency casting director for the part of a business executive and you go dressed in light blue slacks, a sport shirt, and a blazer, the caster is not going to say to himself: "Now, I'll try to imagine this fellow dressed in a pinstripe suit with a conservative shirt and tie, and wearing glasses." Why should he, when the next auditionee is wearing a pinstriped suit, a conservative shirt and tie, and has a pair of glasses with him? You may think, "My great ability and charisma will win me the part no matter how I am dressed. I'm going golfing after the audition and I don't want to bother to change." The trouble is, the next fellow up may have as much ability and charisma as you, but he is dressed for the audition. He's *also* going golfing afterward, but he *is* going to bother to change. (By the way, it is a good idea to have a pair of glasses—just the frames, no lenses—so you can change your look when you want to.)

If you're reading for the part of a nurse, wear a white dress; for a bank teller, a business suit. Don't go to a high-fashion job in denims, or audition for a housewife part in high-fashion clothes (even though you're dying to show them off!) Don't wear theatrical makeup for a housewife role. Don't go in a leather jacket for the part of an insurance salesman, or in a three-button suit for that of a hardhat construction worker. Dress the part as well as you can.

Also, try to find out what the character in the script is doing. You are to be a housewife. But what is she doing? Scrubbing the floor? Shopping? Lunching with friends? You would dress differently for each occasion.

Your Arrival

Arrive at the audition fifteen to thirty minutes ahead of time. Have your photo with you. First, sign in. The sign-in sheet may have a space for you to indicate the time of your actual call as well as your time of arrival. If a union has jurisdiction in your area, there is a rule that you may not be kept waiting for more than an hour without being paid a fee. If you fill in the time of your appointment with your actual arrival time (which is early), you may be at the audition for more than an hour. In that case the ad agency (or auditioner) would be unfairly charged because you arrived early and signed in incorrectly. This is not the way to endear yourself to auditioners so that they will want to call you again. So adjust your arrival time accordingly.

You've come early. You've signed in. You'll be given a script. You now have time to study your script. Start right away to work on it. Don't waste valuable time chatting with others who may be there for the audition. First analyze the copy. Be sure you know what you are saying. Now apply your reading techniques, which we will discuss in detail later. Mark your copy if this helps you. Read the copy aloud a few times until you are satisfied you have the right flow. As you deliver your lines, do not look at anything that will distract you, such as another person. Exclude your surroundings by concentrating on a spot on the wall. Now—but not until now—start to memorize. If you memorize without doing the above, if you memorize by rote, your reading is going to sound that way. If you have marked your copy with places for eye contact and use the speak-read method, you should give a good performance even if you have not thoroughly memorized the copy.

Your work on your script may be interrupted by the auditioner entering the waiting room and saying, "OK, you're next, Mrs. Ross." You see, often those auditioning will be called in the order they signed in instead of the order of their appointments. You signed in early, so now you're being called before the set time. Just say, "I was called for ten o'clock, but I came a little early so I could look over the script." If there are others waiting to audition, say: "I'm in no hurry. Maybe someone else would like to go ahead of me." You'll almost always find someone to take you up on that—someone who *is* in a hurry. Some performers have even resorted to taking the script to the washroom to study so they will be sure to have time to memorize at least part of it before going in for their audition.

By the way, try to keep your script after the audition. This will give you a chance to work on it if you should get a "call back" (a second audition set at another day). You will usually find that there is a pile of scripts. Ask: "May I mark my script?" If the answer is "yes," you will know that there are scripts available for all. If the answer is "no," that means that your script will be given to someone else when you have finished. In that case, copy the script in longhand, or record it if you have a small tape recorder.

While you're waiting to audition, your picture will be collected. Often a Polaroid picture will be taken of you, as well, because your formal photograph may not be up to date, or it may have been glamorized. The auditioners want to see how you *really* look *now*.

Many times you will get a storyboard to look at as well as a script to look over.

The Storyboard

The storyboard is a series of drawings, one for each scene, depicting the principal action of the scene and where it takes place—outdoors, in a kitchen, on a plane, etc. Those who have planned the commercial have outlined to the artist the general age and appearance of the characters involved, and then the artist is given free rein. It may cause the actor some consternation, if he is given a storyboard to look at, to discover that he looks very little like the character as drawn by the artist. Don't let this throw you. Agencies have been known to change the concept of a character if they have been greatly impressed by an auditionee. Also remember that the person who looks most like the drawing is not necessarily the best actor, and they're certainly not going to sacrifice a good performance in the commercial because someone happens to look exactly like the artist's drawing.

The storyboard is useful in giving the actor an idea of what is happening in the scene. Remember, though, the storyboard shows how the commercial is to be *shot,* and it is impossible for you to show all that action in an audition. The drawings just give you the general "feel" of the commercial.

OLDER MAN: Call your wife and kids. I'll meet you downstairs.

YOUNGER MAN: Jimmy, it's Dad.

OLDER MAN: She needs me.
VO: And the more they need you, the more you need Helping Hand.

you get used to being away from the family.

OLDER MAN'S WIFE: Everything's fine but the TV. I'm glad you went to the bank before you left.

something to make sure you don't let them down . . . even if you're not around anymore.

For one out of four hundred Americans, that something is the Hand.

ANNCR: (VO) Helping Hand.

OLDER MAN: After a while on the road . . .

OLDER MAN: Hi, dear. How's everything?

VO: And the more he needs you, the more you need Helping Hand.

ANNCR: (VO) Helping Hand. (SFX) The Hand. When other people count on you, you need something to count on . . .

CHORUS: Get the Hand.

Health
Home
Auto

ANNCR: (VO) For life, health, auto, home . . .

YOUNG MAN: I miss my wife and kid.

MAN: Be back on Tuesday.

(CHUCKLES, TO CAMERA)
He needs me.

OLDER MAN: (TO CAMERA)
VO: And the more they need you, the more you need Helping Hand.

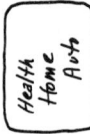

YOUNGER MAN: (HAPPILY) They need me.

KID: Dad, I can't go to camp if you don't pay them by Wednesday.

OLDER MAN: What's the good news from home?

The lines that fit each scene are underneath the drawing of that scene. Sometimes there may be just a few words in one scene, or no words at all. This cuts up the dialogue of the commercial and makes it difficult at times to give a smooth delivery. If you have to read from a storyboard, therefore, study it well. In most instances the storyboard is shown to you just for your information, and you will have a script or a cue card to refer to when you audition.

The storyboard also may be helpful in giving you a clue as to how you will be "shot" at the audition—what your "frame" will be.

Cue Cards

In most instances, when you are auditioning, your script will be block printed on large cardboards. These are cue cards, known in the trade as "idiot cards." They may be positioned above, below, or on either side of the lens. They are widely used for on-camera auditions and sometimes at the actual filming or taping.

When it is your turn to audition, read the card to yourself before your first rehearsal. As with the TelePrompTer, the script, printed in large, block letters, will look much different than the script you read in the waiting room. If the casting director immediately asks if you are ready for a rehearsal, just say, "I'd like to read it down once, first." He or she won't object. Note any differences between script and card wording—sometimes a few words may be changed.

When you rehearse, remember the places where your eyes had to leave the lens, and go to the card. Then do the take exactly the way you rehearsed it. Don't try to stretch your memorization. That will mean you will have to go back to the card at a different place, and it may take you too long to find it.

If you blow a line, either let it go (if it is not an important mistake), or go back and casually make the correction. Above all, don't lose your cool.

What if you stumble? It happens, even with the most experienced performers. If you misread a word that does not seem to you to be important, don't bother to stop to correct it. Just keep on going. If it is important go back to make the correction. But in either case, don't let it upset you. Keep your cool. Don't apologize by saying, "I'm sorry." Don't even *look* apologetic. Don't let your mistake throw you. You will be judged by your overall performance and if you allow a mistake to interrupt the flow of your reading, you will seem amateurish.

Review these steps:

- Memorize by noting the logical sequence and the "sections" of the commercial.
- Decide where you are going to "go to the card."
- When you look at the card, appear to be "thinking" of what you are going to say next, or try to portray whatever emotion you are using while looking at the card. Then look up and say it. Do not read while you are looking at the card!

Remember, the card is there to "throw you a cue," not to give you the whole script.

You're on!

The door to the audition room opens and a voice says, "You're next, Mrs. Ross." You go into the room.

It is generally a rather small room. There are lights, a camera, a "deck" (video tape recorder), and a "monitor" (which looks exactly like your TV set).

The number of people you will meet there varies. It may be only the person doing the auditioning. It will be his or her job to get the best performance possible from you, so remember, it is not going to be you against the auditioner. It's you against the material. The auditioner wants you to be very good—to interpret the material even better than the writer dreamed anyone could. You see, the auditioner seldom makes the final judgment on your performance. The recorded video tape will be played back for a number of people in the agency or production house. If you are good, you're going to make the auditioner look good.

A cameraperson and people who represent the client may be present. You will be introduced and if the product has been on the market, you may be asked, "Are you familiar with our product?" or "Do you use our product?"

Answer "yes," if you do, but don't overdo it. Don't become rapturous. If you've never heard of it, don't say you've used it. It may be something that has not yet been released for sale.

Now for the actual audition. Some auditions consist only of the following procedure: "Just stand in front of the camera and tell us about yourself . . . not your commercial work . . . just about you . . . where you're from . . . what you like . . . your background."

You can use some of the information you used in your interview for the agent, but now you should be more chatty and informal. Be brief, humorous, warm, and friendly. The camera has now become the person you're talking to. Think of it that way, not a cold, inanimate object staring at you. Smile at it. Turn on your personality, but don't gush. Overdoing will make you appear nervous and insecure. Think of something to say that will catch their interest. Maybe you're an archery expert. Maybe you pilot your own plane. Lead with a statement that will make them remember you. (Don't say you are a model; models have a reputation for not being able to act. Say, "I'm an actress, but I occasionally do some modeling.")

If you are to read copy, you will be given brief instructions. Be sure you understand them. It is better to say, "Would you mind repeating that?" than jumping in, doing your take, and then having to do another because you didn't follow instructions.

You will be shown where to stand—most auditions are done standing. When you have taken your position, do not move from it. The cameraperson is trying to get you in the shot. If you move, even so much as to shift your weight, the camera has to follow you, and you are wasting the valuable time of the auditioner and demonstrating that you are not a pro.

You may be reading from cue cards, or perhaps from a script. In the latter case you will not want the script to be seen in the shot. If you cannot see the monitor, ask if the script is out of the shot. Now hold the script flat and directly in front of you. If you do not, you will be seen moving your head every time you look down to get your line. Holding the script high and flat will allow you to see your lines by merely glancing down. Dropping the head to read the line and then raising it to deliver the line becomes distracting. Furthermore, the up-and-down action disrupts the flow of the commercial. If you observe the above suggestions, any head movement you make will be meaningful and will add to the effectiveness of your presentation.

Giving the Slate

"Slate" means identification. The term is derived from the earliest of motion pictures, when a slate was actually held in front of the camera with the scene number written on it in chalk. In an on-camera audition you will give a vocal slate, and it's very important how you do it. Your slate is your vocal and visual calling card. It is the first impression you make. It should not be done casually, sloughed off as if it were unimportant. It is the beginning of your performance and should be delivered with the same care as any line in your script.

Look directly into the lens, smile, and then with all the assurance in the world, say your name. Implied in the way you say your name should be: "I'm glad to be here and I'm about to give you a very good audition." Then hold your expression for a count of two.

An actress who has done many commercials returned to the Weist-Barron School in New York, where she had studied, and said, "There's one thing I learned in class that has won me many a commercial, and that's how to slate. When I turn on my smile and give my name, I've got it made!" She had a great personality and a great smile, and we're sure she wasn't exaggerating.

The inexperienced performer often fails to take the brief pause after the slate before starting the commercial. The pause is important for two reasons. It gives the slate a chance to register effectively, and it gives the performer a moment to change the mood for the first line of the commercial. If you go right from your slate into the copy you may find that you are halfway through the commercial before you have established the proper mood.

Rarely does the mood of your slate match the mood you are trying to bring to the commercial. Let's say, for example, that you have smiled and have given a warm, friendly, positive slate. Then your first line is, "Do you suffer from painful, itching skin?" Your smile doesn't fit the first line, does it? But if you stop momentarily between your slate and the first line, it gives you a chance to "shift gears." The expression for the slate is warm and friendly; the expression that fits the first line is sympathetic, concerned, questioning.

What should you say when you slate? Some actors just give their names; other precede the name with "hello" or hi." Some add the name of the product: "I'm John Jackson for Ivory Soap." Don't say,

"My name is John Jackson," or you'll sound like a contestant on the famous TV show, *To Tell the Truth*!

Know Your Frame

The TV camera is taking a picture of you, but what does that picture include? Just your head and shoulders? Your full figure? It is important that you know. Your gestures and your vocal projection, your whole performance will depend upon the shot. Let us say you are holding up a product and you are in a head and shoulder shot. If the product is not held high enough and is too far away from the body, it will not be in the shot. Hold the product *above* the shoulder line and within the body line and it will be seen. If you cannot see the monitor, ask the cameraperson where you are being cut, and imagine that you are in a picture frame. Since the TV tube is slightly wider than it is high, you have a little more latitude in the width than in the height. A good way to practice your gestures within shots is to stand in front of a mirror and with your hands measure the distance from the top of your head to a point slightly below your shoulders. Now spread your hands to the side, increasing the distance slightly, and you have your frame. Practice gestures within that frame. Follow the same procedure for a waist shot. You will, of course, discover that the gestures now can be broader. Be careful that your gestures do not "pop in" to the shot from below. They will distract from your performance. Let the viewer see them start.

If you are holding up a prop, such as the product, in a waist shot, center the prop in your frame and hold it close to or within the body line. Remember that the camera is shooting only half of you, so if the prop is held away from the body it will seem to be twice as far away from you as it is in actuality.

The head and shoulder shot and the waist shot are the two most generally used in an audition. If you are in a full-length shot you need not be concerned about your gestures. They will all be in the shot.

Body Movements

Nothing can be more distracting than weaving back and forth in a head and shoulder shot. The playback may even show your head going partially out of the frame. The cameraperson cannot possibly anticipate your movements, but even if the camera follows you, your performance will have a nonprofessional appearance. To make certain that you do not move laterally, stand firmly on your feet. Pivotal movements can be made, but do not move from side to side.

When the camera (or zoom lens) pulls back and shows more of your body, in TV parlance it is called a "wider" shot or a "looser" shot. Now you should incorporate some body movement, or the shot will look static, and you will appear stiff. The farther back the camera pulls, the more body movement you should use.

Can I Ask for a Shot?

Yes, most certainly, but the cameraperson may not always comply with your request. The agency representative may have given instructions that everyone is to be photographed in the same way. But if no such instructions have been given, changing your shot means only moving the zoom lens to tighten or loosen the shot.

Vocal Projection Should Match the Shot

Vocal and video perspective should match. I'm sure you have seen a scene in a movie where two players are conversing in a fairly close shot. They then move across the street while the camera remains fixed, but the sound perspective has not changed with the picture. You can hear them just as loudly as when they were close to the camera. It seems false, because the vocal perspective and the picture do not match. If you don't know your shot, you may be giving too little or too much projection.

Whether we are aware of it or not, we see each other in different shots, depending upon our proximity to the other person. I see a friend walking down the street. I see him full length. I call out to him, "Hello, Joe, how are you?" Now let's change the scene. I meet Joe at a cocktail party face to face, barely two feet from me. If I address him at the same volume as I did on the street, he'll back away from me, thinking I've suddenly gone deaf, since deaf people often speak too loudly.

At the cocktail party I see Joe in a head and shoulder shot. To see him full length I would have to lower my head, panning down his figure. When you are in a head and shoulder shot on camera you must imagine that the person you are addressing is just across the mike from you—about two or three feet away—and you must adjust your volume accordingly without letting your energy or enthusiasm drop.

When you are in a waist shot you can imagine that you are talking to someone who is eight to ten feet from you. Now you use more projection. A full-length shot (rarely used at an audition) calls for even more projection. But never shout, unless instructed to do so.

What if the Shot Changes During My Audition?

This may happen. The camera may start on a close-up and pull back to a waist shot, or vice versa. If you have asked about the shot or shots prior to the delivery of your copy, you will be prepared. If the opening shot is a close-up, such as a head and shoulder shot, and then the shot is widened to a waist shot, you would slightly *increase* your volume. The reverse is true: If the opening shot is a waist shot and the camera pulls in to a close-up, you must slightly *decrease* your volume, or it will seem that you are talking too loudly. You must, of course, determine in advance at what point in the script the shot changes, so you can adjust your volume accordingly.

Matching Your Physical Performance to the Shot

Just as your volume should match the shot, so must your physical performance. Intense facial expressions which may be effective in a longer shot may look greatly overdone and even ludicrous in a close-up. Conversely, a subtle expression may register very effectively in a close-up and be completely lost in a longer shot. We have previously mentioned body movement. Remember, more in a long shot, less in a close-up.

Garson Kanin, the author and playwright, reported on a talk show that he had once been permitted on the set when Greta Garbo was shooting a film. After the long shots had been photographed and the set was being relighted for the closeups, Kanin observed Garbo off in a corner talking to herself. After the shooting was finished he asked her what she had been doing in those minutes before the shooting resumed. "I was rehearsing my close-ups," she said. "The great Garbo rehearsing close-ups!" said Kanin on the talk show. "You'd think they'd just turn the camera on her and that would be that."

If the shots were a concern to Garbo, let them be to you too. Don't just "wing it." You may think you are gorgeous and talented and you'll knock them over. Perhaps you're right, but waiting to audition after you is someone who is also gorgeous and talented but has the technique to go with it. Who do you think will win the audition?

Handling Props—Gestures—Pantomime

A producer/director from Ogilvy & Mather, a large New York advertising agency, once stressed the importance of handling props well and of using good gestures and effective pantomimes in auditions. "I hold many auditions," he said. Then he added, "Let us say I have two auditionees who seem to be equal in many respects. Both look the part, both have great charisma, both give superlative readings of the commercial. One handles the props with authority, uses effective gestures, and employs well-thought-out and representational pantomime. The other is sloppy in handling props, just waves the air to gesture, and make no effort to create pictures with his pantomime. Who is going to win the audition?" The answer is fairly obvious, isn't it?

The word "props" (short for "properties") is borrowed from the theater. Props are anything handled during a performance—a glass, a cigarette, the product (when doing a commercial). You are often asked to use props during an audition. Perhaps the only prop may be the product.

Before you start reciting the text of a commercial, handle the props—get the feel of them. Be sure you are holding the prop so that if there is lettering on it, it can be read on camera. Be sure you do not hold the prop awkwardly. Now practice the moves you will make as you demonstrate the prop.

If you are given specific directions, be sure you follow them explicitly and are able to repeat them—not *almost* as you were told, but *exactly*. You may not find this easy at first. If you were rehearsing for a play, even in a small part, you would probably have a few weeks to assimilate the action and your use of the props. These few weeks are condensed into a few minutes when you are auditioning or actually shooting a commercial.

At first you may encounter a psychological block as you try to remember all of your directions. I'm sure you've all had the experience of stopping your car along the road to get directions. Your informant says, "Just go down to the third light, make a left on Route 25. Go about a half a mile and make a left on Water Street [etc.]." By this time you're saying to yourself, "I can't remember all this. I just won't remember." Of course you could remember, if you really concentrated, but because the directions came at you so fast, you erected a mental block.

To discipline yourself to overcome a mental block, get someone to give you directions when you are practicing at home. Force yourself to remember the directions, and carry them out accurately.

Back to the audition. You have been given the directions. Now coordinate the words and action. Be sure you occasionally make visual reference to the product. Really look at it—not just in its direction.

Pick up the props and place them down noiselessly. Don't bang them down. It will distract from your presentation. The microphone seems to magnify the sounds you make, and on playback even rather discreet sounds may give your reading heavy punctuations and interruptions.

If you have to twist the top off a bottle, be sure you have loosened the top beforehand so it will come off easily, but never put your prop on "a hair trigger." That means loosening the top to the extent that the slightest movement such as moving it or picking it up will send the top flying. To remove a top, or to place one back on quickly, turn the top in one direction with one hand, and turn the bottle in the other direction.

When shooting a commercial you will have to be more exact handling props than at an audition, although, as we have pointed out, the more precisely you use the props at an audition the better chance you have of winning the commercial. At a shoot you may be required to bring the prop up to an exact position every time without looking at it, because your eyes are on the lens. To do this you must use your "peripheral vision"—what you see out of the corner of your eye when you are looking straight ahead.

First you will be told where the prop should be held. Now hold the prop in the correct position and, as you look at the lens, with your peripheral vision line up the prop with some object in the studio. You now have established an "air mark" so that each time you pick up the prop it will be in the same position.

In conclusion, make sure the prop is going to work. Put it down and pick it up without looking, to be sure you have it in the right position every time. Don't cover the label with your fingers. Hold it from behind. If you are showing a prop to the camera, hold it up level, but be careful not to cover your face.

This is it!

You get a cue from your auditioner and you begin. Talk to one person. TV is a very personal medium. It is not like the stage. You are not addressing an audience. You are speaking just to one person—to that person seated in a living room watching the TV screen. You are a guest in that person's home in a one-to-one medium, so modulate your voice. Don't shout. People resent being shouted at.

Although your voice should be conversational in tone, do not drop your energy level. Some actors, in an attempt to be conversational, reduce their enthusiasm, with the result that they do not sound convincing. It is better to "come on big." Any casting person is happy to "push" an extrovert back, but few will bother to "pull" an introvert forward. So, at least on your first reading, give your most enthusiastic (but natural) performance.

Exude confidence as you audition. Bear in mind that the advertising agency people want to hire winners. They want to believe that you know what you're doing, that you are the professional, that you are there to show them how the commercial should be read. Make them believe with your reading that if they hire you, the commercial will be a success.

After the reading, do not make editorial or facial comments on your own work. In politics, we often hear that "TV is the most powerful unmasker of fraudulent personalities that has ever been developed." People can see on the TV screen (by observing your face) what's on your mind. For this reason, after you have finished reading the commercial, retain the facial expression with which you ended, until they say "cut." Don't make a face that says, "That was lousy, wasn't it?" Auditioners are only too willing to agree with you. They don't need your assistance to find fault.

Years ago the Jam Handy Company in Detroit was one of the most prominent producers of industrial films in the country. Their salesmen were all trained to turn to a potential client after a sample screening (when the lights came up) and say, "Now, wasn't that a *really great* picture!" That's what your face should say (if anything)—"Now, wasn't that a *really great* take?"—even if it wasn't.

Points to Remember

- Match your vocal projection to your frame. Close-up: less voice. Waist shot: more voice.
- Look at the camera as if it were a person. Hold your script in a position to be able to do this without bobbing your head. If there is a cue card, refer to it infrequently, and don't talk while looking at it.
- Move your head at transitions.
- Use a conversational voice, not a stage voice.
- Don't "get set" physically—stay loose.
- As you subtract "the voice" from your performance, add more facial expressions to make up for it. Fit the expression to the dialogue.
- Don't be a "Johnny One-Note"—let your voice ride up and down.
- Learn the first and the last line well, so you will be talking directly into the lens when you say those lines. First and last impressions are important.
- Back your script with a clipboard so if your hands shake, it will not be as noticeable.
- Be yourself—not "an announcer."
- Think of each audition as just another practice-learning experience and you won't get so "up tight."

Auditioning Two in a Scene (Doubles)

In the reception room you will be given a script and told which of two parts you will be playing. If partners are assigned in advance, it is a good idea to read the scene with your partner prior to your audition. It will give you an idea of what your partner is going to do so you can prepare your reactions. If partners are not assigned (and they may not be until the actual audition), memorize as much of the script as you can. You will not have as much to learn as when you are auditioning alone. These days, commercials seldom run longer than thirty seconds, and since a thirty-second commercial is actually only twenty-eight seconds in length, you'll have about fourteen seconds of copy to learn if the lines are fairly evenly divided, and you should be able to become very familiar with the copy while you're awaiting your turn.

Once in the audition room you will be told where to stand. You should stand close to your partner, so there are only a few inches dividing you. This allows the cameraperson to close in on a waist shot. Two people standing side by side in a waist shot will fill the frame. If you are standing more than a few inches apart, the zoom lens will have to pull back and your face will not be as large on the screen.

You should stand facing the camera with your feet actually pointed at the lens. Now turn your head until you just see your partner. Your head will now be in a three-quarter position, allowing you both to see your partner and glance at the cue card if you need to. In the three-quarter position the camera will see more of your face than if your profile is to the camera.

Avoid looking down. The lighting for an audition is almost always very rudimentary—a light shooting straight at you, or perhaps a light higher than your head and shooting down on you. In either case, if you drop your head, shadows will be cast on your eyes. If you are a woman with bangs, you have to be particularly careful. Even if you do not drop your head, your bangs may cast a shadow, so you must shorten your bangs or push them aside when you audition.

When holding a product and looking at it, hold it chest high or higher—not waist high, or you'll be burying your head to look at it.

Although you'll be using the three-quarter position when addressing your partner, find motivations in the script that will allow you to look away from your partner—more in the direction of the lens. A reaction may motivate a turn away from your partner, or perhaps an idea strikes you, or you start a line toward your partner and then turn slightly toward the camera, as if formulating what you want to say. It will look more natural than holding all the way through the dialogue in the three-quarter position. Remember, if someone is speaking to us and never varies his gaze by occasionally looking away, it makes us feel uncomfortable.

Stand on an even keel with your partner. Do not allow your partner to get farther away from the camera than you are. In show biz the expression is, "Don't let an actor upstage you." If you are "upstaged," you may find yourself turning to talk to your partner, and all the camera will see is the back of your head. Don't let your partner upstage you vocally. Match his or her vocal level. If you speak more softly than the other person, you will come across as having less energy, and it may cause you to lose your audition.

Look at the cue card as little as possible. Remember, a small flub is better than destroying your relationship or contact with your partner, because a look at a cue card comes over as just that, and it's very obvious to the auditioner. If you are working from a script, the script will probably be on a music stand in front of you. Don't look down at it unless you are really lost. Again, it will break the contact with your partner. Some actors keep looking down just to check to see if they are reading every line correctly. Don't do it. Have confidence in your memorization.

Pick up your cues. Don't leave spaces between your partner's lines and your lines. Listen to your partner, and react to what is being said. Your lines must "play off" what your partner is saying. If your partner is not as good an actor as you are, don't let it worry you. The selection of performers is seldom made by pairs, but by individual performances. If you are the better actor, your performance will "shine" in contrast.

Slating for doubles is generally done in the following manner: The zoom lens will take a close-up shot of the person on the right (camera left). The auditioner will point to that person and ask him or her to slate. Now the camera will move to the next person to take that close-up and again the auditioner will ask for a slate. Be sure you wait for your cue to slate. Sometime the auditioner will just say, "OK, slate it," assuming that both the auditionees know the procedure. In that case, if you are the second person to slate, be sure you see the camera move to you and stop. If you slate while the camera is moving toward you, you won't be in the picture. They'll hear your voice, but the picture will be of a blank wall—the space between you and your partner.

After the last line of the commercial the auditioner may want both of you to look at the lens with a reaction. If so, be sure you hold your reaction until you know that the scene is over. You'll hear the recorder stopping, or the auditioner will say something like, "Thanks" or "OK, that's it."

A final reminder: Use the full-profile position very sparingly, if at all. Remember, "Your face is your fortune". Let them see it!

After the Audition

You have finished the audition. If you have been faithfully using the techniques outlined in this book you should have acquitted yourself creditably. A few do's and don'ts. First the don'ts. If they smile after your audition and say, "Great!" don't assume you've got the job. Since you were competing against good performers, all of you were probably "great."

Don't worry over some little "glitch" you made. The overall performance is what you'll be judged by. Don't go home and nervously sit by the phone waiting for a call. The video tape made at the audition will be given to the ad agency and must be reviewed by the account executive, sometimes in consultation with the client. It may be a few days before a decision is reached.

Do say to yourself, "I gave a good audition (if you have), and I can be proud of my performance. If I don't win this one, I'll get the next one." Do review your performance, and if there were spots you think could have been improved, make a mental note of them. This can improve your next audition.

Now one of three things will happen: You will receive no call. That means you did not win. (Very seldom will you be called to be told you did not win.) You will receive a "call-back." You will be put on "first refusal."

What is a call-back? Many times the agency or client has difficulty choosing among a few very good auditionees, so they will call you back for another audition, sometimes using the same script, sometimes an entirely different one. If you have taken the original script with you when you left the studio, or copied it or recorded it, brush up on it now, before you take the second audition. If you get a *second* call-back and you are a union member you must be paid the actor's hourly rate as provided in the contract, but very seldom will you receive a second call-back. When money is involved, the agency or client usually finds it easier to make a decision without calling back performers.

First refusal means that you and usually a few others are being considered for the role. Since the casting people can't make up their minds about a final choice, they ask you for a first refusal. If you grant it, and usually you do, you must then let them know immediately if you are being considered for a competing product. Then it is up to the agency either to hire you or release you. In actual practice, an actor is seldom so lucky as to be considered for two competing products within a short span of time, so if you get a first refusal, just pat yourself on the back. Now you *will* be nervously awaiting a phone call. Generally on a first refusal you will be informed whether you are hired or released.

Memorizing for Auditions

"Should I try to memorize the copy for an audition?" Yes, but in your delivery don't try to depend entirely on memorization. Memorization helps you to retain not only the words but also the way you are going to deliver those words, so you are not so likely to change your delivery once you are auditioning. And, of course, the more you have memorized, the more you will be able to keep your eyes on the lens. But—it is much better to refer to the cue cards or your script now and then than to fight to remember words, because that effort will show in your eyes, and your auditioner will see that you are valiantly trying to recall the script. If you practice at home "getting up from the script"—raising your eyes when you speak—and when you are auditioning, you remember to get your eyes up and hold for a count of one at the copy points, you should be able to give an effective audition.

On the Job

In the Film Studio

The telephone rings. You answer it. And congratulations, you've got the job! You've won the commercial! You will be informed of the day of shooting. If you have lines, you will receive a script a few days in advance. Memorize it well. On the set you will discover that the commercial will be broken down into scenes. You will have to deliver only a few lines, or even only one line, at a time, so you may ask, "Then why bother to memorize?" As we have pointed out, memorization is not only setting the words in your mind but also fixing the way you are going to deliver them. Under the pressure of filming it is very easy to forget; you want to be solid in your lines and your delivery.

You will be told what clothing to bring. If special costuming is involved, an appointment will be set up for a fitting.

On the day of the shooting be sure you arrive *on time*. If it is a union contract, find out if you are going to get an additional fee for having supplied your own clothing. If you are entitled to the fee and it is not so specified in your contract, call this to the attention of the person who handed you your contract.

Now you will go to "makeup," and if you are a woman, a hairdresser will give the final touches to your coiffure. Next, into the clothes you will wear, if not the ones you have on. In any event, your clothes will be checked by the costumer.

When they have finished "dolling you up," you make your way to the sound stage. Here you will find yourself in the midst of a bustle of activity—lights being set up, the camera operator using a meter to check the intensity of the light, carpenters pounding away making last-minute adjustments to the set. You will encounter a number of people with whom you will have little or no direct contact during the shooting. There will be the sound crew. If you are to speak in a fixed position or are "body miked," there may be just one sound person. If you have to move to different positions and if other actors are involved, the crew usually consists of three sound technicians. One engineer will "mix" the sound on what appears to be an ordinary tape recorder (but costs three thousand dollars). Another will adjust the microphone and follow a script to see when he should point the mike toward you, and when he should change its position to pick up a person playing opposite you. A third will push the boom on which the mike person is standing (if he or she is standing on one).

There are also "grips," the stagehands of film and videotape. Then there are the "prop" people. They seek out and rent all the furnishings for the set and cause them to be placed in the proper position. They are usually supervised by a set designer.

All of these groups think of themselves as departments: the Sound Department, the Grip Department, etc.

There is also the Electrical Department. These people walk the catwalks and adjust the lights under the supervision of the head electrician, called the gaffer, or the gaff. The camera operator gives lighting instructions to the gaff, who then tells the crew how to adjust the lights.

The Camera Department in New York (and usually elsewhere as well) consists of the camera operator and an assistant. In Hollywood, there would be three: the camera operator, an assistant, and their boss, the director of cinematography. The first two do the actual work; the director of cinematography, who is considered a creative artist, is the only one of the three who gets top billing in the film.

The camera operator in consultation with the director shoots the scenes. The assistant loads the camera, unloads it, focuses it, and cleans it.

You will also find that the copywriter is on the set, in case there are changes to be made in the script. Present as well will be the art director and the agency film (or videotape) producer. The agency producer is the businessperson of the outfit, riding herd on the budget and following up on all the details of the production. He or she may or may not have any creative say in the production, because today, in ad agencies, the "creative team" has more and more to say and the producer less and less. Also, the account executive may take time out to be present at the shooting. Many times the client—a representative of the manufacturer, usually the advertising manager—feels his or her presence is essential should some matter of company policy come up during the shooting requiring his or her wisdom and authority.

With all these people on the set, there is bound to be a lot of noise and confusion. Finally (and it may be a couple of hours) "the tumult and the shouting dies," and it's time for a rehearsal and a take.

The director will outline the action and you will run through the scene a few times. A timing will be taken each time. Timing is very important. In the filming, a retake may be required if the shot is even one-half second too long or too short.

Now we're ready for the "take." The assistant cameraperson strings out a tape measure from the lens to your nose to set the exact distance on the lens. The director calls for quiet, and you hear the sound of "the bells," which commands quiet not only on the set, but also in any adjoining rooms where sound might be picked up by the mike. All is silent except for the soft thump, thump. That's your heart.

The director says, "Roll sound."

When the sound engineer's tape recorder is moving at the proper speed, he or she will call out "Speed." The director then says, "Roll the camera." When the camera is operating at the proper speed, the camera operator will say "Speed." The director then says, "Sticks in," or "Slate in."

At this point, one of the crew steps in front of the camera and gives the name of the visual take—"Take one, Scene one"—and the sound take number (which is usually quite different) and steps out. Now the director will cue you by saying "Action."

Start at the word "Action" and don't stop until the director says "Cut." Too many actors take it upon themselves (when they make what they deem to be a mistake) to yell "Cut!" and start apologizing. Don't do this. The mistake you made may be preferable to the original idea, and you may have just ruined it by yelling "Cut!" You are no director, so wait until you hear "Cut" before you stop.

"Cut," says the director, and the take is over. If the take was a good one, the director may say, "Print," or "That's a buy." You would be very lucky if the first take pleased everyone. You may have been great, but the timing may have been slightly off. The director might want to change the lighting. There could be one of a dozen reasons to reshoot the scene. The most common one comes from the director, who says, "I think we can get a better one."

Now let us introduce you to the script girl. She has been sitting quietly in a chair near the set, timing the scene and taking notes. She'll tell you with which hand you picked up the box and remind you of every move you made. All this information is important as the shooting progresses from scene to scene. You see, the shots must match. For example you cannot pick up a box with the right hand and in the next scene put it down with the left.

The script girl will also remind you of the position you were in when the shot ended, not that you should need reminding. A pro remembers all those details. It is the mark of a pro to be able to remember everything he or she did in a shot and do it exactly the same way every time the scene is shot. If you do not repeat the action in the close shot the same way you did it in the long shot, the shots will not "intercut." So be a pro—do it the same way every time. When they cut from a long shot to a medium shot, your clothing must be arranged the same way, your pen must be in the same pocket, your legs must be crossed the same way. If you forget, the script girl will check you.

Incidentally, don't help the grips or prop people by doing their job for them—moving a chair, for instance. It will not be appreciated and will stamp you as a neophyte. You will be infringing on their responsibilities under their union rules. The only props you should handle are your personal props—your pen, your glasses, the product, etc.—the ones you are supposed to handle in the shot.

Well, the first scene was a "buy," and while they're setting up for the next shot, relighting, etc., you can review your lines for the coming scene.

On the set (when you're not acting) the assistant director (the AD) is your boss. He or she tells you when to go to lunch, when to return, if you're needed the next day, if you can get off for an hour to go to another audition (and you sometimes can). If you do get off, don't, for heaven's sake, be late returning. And since you will usually be needed exactly when you're not around, let the AD know where you plan to be if you leave the set to go to the washroom or for any reason, so you can be found when you are needed.

Remember, too, that although extras are hired through an agent on the first day, the ones who come back for another day or days during the shoot are usually called by the AD. So be nice to that individual, who can get you more work.

Finally, since it is the AD's job to arrange the production shooting to save money, recording voice-over lines, when your face is not on the screen, may be saved up until the end of the day, when the full crew and other actors have been dismissed. These are called "wild lines," and you will usually be asked to read them all at once. When you do, don't bury your head in the script, and don't use a different mike position from the one you used earlier when you were speaking on camera. If you do, the quality of the sound will be different, and when the lines are cut together, they may not match.

To summarize, on the set: Be on time; know your lines; keep quiet and learn by observation; don't leave without asking permission; don't try to direct the picture by yelling "Cut!" when you make a mistake; and be friendly in a quiet, professional way.

There is no substantial difference between filming and videotaping, except that you will get your orders at a taping from the stage manager, who receives his from the director over the intercom that he wears in his ear. You will also hear directions given over the horn—the speaker. The stage manager usually signals for action by pointing to you.* You may have to learn on what line you will turn from Camera 1 to Camera 2 or 3, etc. The directors of videotape are now working more closely with actors than they used to but are still physically positioned in a control room, which can be five floors above you, at the back of the stage, or in a truck down the block. Tape directors usually watch the action over monitors, not in person. Of course, for you, as well as for the director or client, the tape can be played back immediately, and changes can be made.

As a final note, try to take a 35mm still camera to the set and ask to have a photo made of you that you can later have made into a postcard to send to agents. The best person to ask to take the picture is the assistant camera operator. Be sure you know what kind of film is in your camera. That's the first thing you'll be asked.

Filming on Location

"On location" refers to filming somewhere other than in a studio. It could be anywhere: a city street, inside or outside someone's home, a

---

*You may be told to take your cue from the light. That means the "tally" light (or lights)—a small red light on the side or top of the camera. When the light is on, it means that the camera is activated and they are shooting the picture.

park, a farm—maybe even in Miami, Florida. Your call may be "weather permitting," which means that because they'll be shooting outdoors the call may be canceled if the weather is bad. In most instances your call will include extra days in case the weather is not right for shooting.

If the filming is to be done a long distance away, you will be paid for travel time, for your traveling expenses (tickets often are bought for you), and for your living expenses while on location.

Let us say the shooting will be done not far from the city where you live. You will be told to meet at a certain spot early in the morning. There all the actors involved will be driven to the location. Of course, you might be able to drive to the location yourself, but the producer wants to make sure that everyone involved in the filming is on tap.

When you arrive at the location you will find that trucks containing camera, sound, and lighting equipment are already at the scene, unloading and setting up for the filming. If you are not already dressed in the clothes you will wear, there will be a van where you can change. Your makeup will be applied, and you're ready to go. Ah, but the crew isn't. It takes a lot of time to set up for exterior shots, so you may find yourself waiting around for an hour or more before the filming starts.

In the meantime you may be "body miked," and you may be asked to run through your lines so the audio engineer can set a level. You will be told to be careful that the microphone (generally strapped around your neck or taped to your chest) is not rubbed against or hit during the recording. It will produce a loud noise on the sound track, and the scene will have to be done over.

When the filming actually starts, the procedure will be much the same as it was in the studio, except that passing planes, trucks, etc., may make noises so loud that a retake is required. Some production companies videotape the scene while it is being filmed, so that it can be played back immediately. If the director thinks the take is a particularly good one as far as action goes, he may keep the take and ask you to dub your line or lines later in an audio studio.

You will get a lunch break. The fare supplied is usually ample and good. Then the filming starts all over again. The thoughtful producer who wants the best out of his actors will have brought along chairs for you to sit on so you can rest between takes. If it is a union production, this is mandatory.

When the filming is over, the director will say, "It's a wrap," and you'll be headed for home, perhaps to go through the same procedure the next day.

If your location is a busy city street, expect to be ogled by passersby. Don't be distracted. Keep your concentration. (Anyhow, it's sort of fun—all that attention. You're a movie star!)

If you are to be in an industrial or educational film, the shooting may be entirely on location and require no studio shots at all. The location would be the plant or offices of the client. Because space there may be limited, it is often not easy to set up equipment, and shooting may take longer. But what do you care, if you're being hired by the day! Again there may be sound problems that will require postdubbing. If you have long pages of dialogue, a TelePrompTer will most likely be provided. It is very difficult to learn pages and pages of dialogue dealing with things unfamiliar to you, but study your script well, so that when you do use the TelePrompTer you won't sound as though you are reading. When shooting an industrial, the producer or director will almost always ask you to read the copy for him or her at a prerehearsal, to acquaint you with all those technical terms that are Greek to you.

Well, you've made your first commercial (or maybe industrial film) either in the studio or on location, and you're slouched down on the sofa watching TV. A commercial comes on. We wonder if you now say, "Boy, that must be easy. *Anybody* could do *that!*"

Voice-Overs

As you probably realize, there is an unseen presence in almost every commercial—the voice of the narrator. This person may have only a tag line, or his or her voice may underscore the entire action on the screen.

The Voice-over Audition

Auditions for voice-overs usually take place in the audio room of an advertising agency or in an independent casting firm. You sign in, just as you did for the on-camera audition, and you will be given a copy of the script. Read it over thoroughly, analyze it, and mark it. Then read it aloud. You needn't do more than say the words under your breath, but it is important actually to articulate the words so that you will not stumble over any of them while you are auditioning.

When you go into the studio you will give a level, and when the tape is rolling you'll be asked to slate. Slate just as you did for the on-camera audition.

Recording a Voice-over

When recording a voice-over, the job is done in a special sound studio. These studios have no camera or lights; they are staffed by sound technicians sitting at control boards. They are usually large, comfortable studios with theaterlike seats.

Often you will be recording a voice-over without seeing the picture it accompanies—recording "wild." But if the photography has been completed, you may be required to "record to picture," and the picture they show you to work with will probably be a "scratch track"—a film that has been cut to time but doesn't have all the final effects such as fade-ins and fade-outs.

They show you the film, and they show it over and over. That's so you can coordinate your voice with the action.

Sometimes you will be told where to start, and it will be in terms of feet of film. There is a footage counter near the screen, and on it will be projected the number of feet that have gone by. So when they tell you "Start at foot 13," you watch the counter; when it reads 13, you begin.

As you do this, you will see that what you are saying does not always go with the action. You may be coming in too early or too late in certain places. Make notes and adjust. Maybe you should start the third line of copy at foot 29 instead of 32, so that you'll be talking about the cute little girl when she is on the screen and not while they are showing a bulldozer operator.

After you have watched the screen and mumbled the script to yourself for a while, they will say, "Shall we try one?" "Why not?" you answer with a professional air. Now they are going to make the first take. You do not slate. The engineer does this on a special microphone. Foot 13 appears, and you begin.

When you have managed to coordinate your voice with the screen action, they usually begin to work on the nuances of the reading. This also takes time. "Please emphasize the word 'stings'." "Don't take so long to say the competitive product name." "Change the word 'hurt' to 'pain' in line 9."

You will see them huddling in the control room, talking (that is, you will if you look over your shoulder). Don't be paranoid. Usually the discussions are about script cuts and other technical matters, not about you or your reading.

Even though you do a good job, don't be surprised to hear someone say, "Take 28." Any spot is frequently recorded . . . and recorded . . . and recorded . . . for a wide variety of reasons. Even if you get a perfect first take, they make changes "in case the client changes his mind" about this, that, or the other line.

Who are the others in the studio? In the master control room (enclosed in glass) there is the engineer, the film editor, the ad agency producer (who may direct the session), the ad agency account executive, the client's representative, the copywriter (in case cuts must be made), and the music editor (in case he made a mistake when he edited the music and sound). In the room with you there may be one to three engineers. Each is sitting behind you at a console. One is setting the levels of the sound track. The second is handling the music track. The third is recording you. The master control is "mixing" the three together on a master tape.

Sometimes an ad agency wants to do the track beforehand (this is always true in camera animation, because the animators must draw the mouth movement to the length of each of your words). If they are recording prior to filming, you will be told when to start and stop by a signal light on your podium. When it goes on, you speak. When it goes off, you shut up. Later the film is shot to correspond with the length of your sentences.

Can you hear the music? Sometimes. They may put "cans" (earphones) on your head. Sometimes they are afraid the sound of the music will "leak" from the cans into your track. Hearing the music is very helpful in giving you the mood for the narration, and you can usually hear it before you begin to record. Occasionally it is played loud enough through the control-room glass to be audible to you.

Incidentally, if your voice track is perfect in every way except for one word or so, they may do a "pickup." You just do the one line involved over again. It is important that the tonal and volume level of the line be the same as for the rest of the spot. Usually they let you hear the spot up to that line, then signal you to deliver it. That way, you know it will match. Just to be sure, however, they don't dismiss you until they cut the new sentence into the tape and listen to it, to be certain it matches.

At VO recordings, it is good to know these terms: The "horn" is a speaker; the "pot" is the device that makes you louder or softer—volume control, in short; "cans" are earphones; the "gain" is how loud or how soft. They will say to an engineer, "Can you up the gain?"

As you know, Americans often record English-language dialogue to foreign films. This is called sync dubbing. You fit your English words into the mouth of an Italian. Some people have great talent for this; others have none. Companies who do this are often willing to try anyone, because being able to do it is sort of a "gift." But note that the term "dubbing" is often used to cover the entire field of voice narration.

It is while doing this kind of VO work that you will begin to appreciate our technique of being able to read the script, watch the screen, and look at your script by only flicking your eyes, rather than bobbing your head up and down. Bobbing the head up and down or turning the head sideways while reading can vary the sound—reducing it slightly when you are away from the mike. Your mike position must remain constant at all times.

Points to Remember

Mike positions are too complex to be discussed more than briefly. However, it is important to remember these points:

When you are "on mike" you can't move your face from side to side to act. You must stay "on the mike." Planting your feet on the floor and not moving them is the best way of assuring yourself that you will not change your position.

Speak across or under the mike rather than directly into it if you are close to it. This will minimize sibilance and "popping" of plosives (which include such sounds as b's and p's and t's). The closer you get to a mike, the better and richer your voice sounds. But all defects also become more apparent.

When you act with someone else, don't turn to speak to him or her. Speak to the mike.

"Presence" means the degree of closeness felt by the listener. If you put your mouth right against the mike, the listener feels that you are "in his (or her) ear." When you speak from a distance, he feels you are "across the room."

Don't make paper noises with your script. If it is two pages long, separate them and carefully slide them apart when the time comes to read the second page.

Don't put your elbows on the table to read, or hit your foot against the table on which the mike is placed; these introduce horrendous noises into the audio track.

Minimize your breathing sounds by opening your mouth wide, as you would for a dentist. With lips almost closed you can hear the intake. (Try it. You'll hear what we mean.)

Stand or sit about ten to twelve inches from the mike. This varies, but use this distance for "openers."

Don't forget: When you give a level, keep on giving it until the engineer says, "OK."

Intimate emotions usually require presence. This could include things pertaining to secrets, babies, sex—so "close in" on the mike.

Saliva noises ("pops" and "clicks" in the mouth) ruin a lot of takes. To get rid of them, take a drink of water. To prevent the buildup of saliva in the first place, be careful of eating or drinking anything prior to your recording. You may find that the studio will offer you a Danish and coffee if it's a morning recording. Politely refuse, or you may find your reading becoming what the "pros" call "slurpy." Water is OK, and hot tea with lemon sometimes will help you get frogs out of your throat.

If there are other people auditioning, let them go first. Say, "I'm in no hurry." It will give you more time to study your script.

If the auditioners play back your first take and ask, "What do you think?" be very honest and very critical. If you liked the take, don't be afraid to say so. It is not bragging. You are offering your objective judgment of your work. Sometimes you will discover things that bother you that your auditioners haven't caught. Point out what you didn't like and say, "I'd like to do it again." If they ask, "Do *you* have any ideas?" try to come up with one. It will show that you're versatile. But unless asked, don't say, "I'd like to try it another way." It will appear that you weren't sure of your first take.

Always try at least to hear your playback. If the auditioner is in a big hurry, he may not offer to do it. But you can always ask, "Have we time to hear a playback?" It's not being presumptuous, it's being a pro.

Confidential or Intimate Delivery

The confidential or intimate delivery can be done only in voice-over because the effect can be produced only very close to the mike. Sometimes this technique is referred to as "over the shouder," as if you were looking over someone's shoulder reporting an "on the spot" happening in a manner and vocal volume to keep those standing near you from hearing you.

This delivery is often called for when you are doing "taste appeal" commercials—those that extol the flavor and aroma of products to titillate the appetite of the viewer. "Ah, the rich flavor and enticing aroma of Cafe Freeze-dried Coffee!" For women it is also a way to make your voice sound "sexy."

To begin with, you will probably have to have a low voice to be effective in this delivery. Your voice will be made to sound even lower as you move toward the mike.

Work three or four inches from the mike, making certain that no exhalation of breath hits it. Watch out particularly for p's and f's, but go easy on all consonants. Talk as if you did not want someone nearby to hear you, using very little volume. Speak in as low a tone (pitch) as you can. Speak at an even rate without rushing words. Keep an even volume. Inflect to get the meaning as you would normally, but cut down on the range of your inflection.

Last, do not let all of these mechanics get in the way of the meaning of what you are saying. When recording a confidential delivery in a voice-over studio, the engineer will help you to get in the exact position to make your delivery most effective.

Timing Voice-over Commercials

If you are reading a commercial properly (and presuming it was written properly, with the correct number of words), you should come in on time.

Unless "time" is a critical factor in the commercial at on-camera auditions, it is seldom taken into account. At voice-over auditions, it is most important, because timing often is very essential, and an actor who gives a good performance in forty-five seconds may fall apart when asked to do a similar performance in only thirty or twenty-eight seconds.

On film in a sixty-second commercial, there are only fifty-eight seconds of dialogue. There can be no more because of the manner in which the film is projected. In a thirty-second film spot, there are twenty-eight seconds of dialogue; in a twenty-second film, eighteen seconds. But on videotape and audiotape, you have the full time. So if you finish a thirty-second film narration in thirty seconds, you are, in reality, two seconds over.

Learning to pace properly so that you finish "on the nose" is a matter of practice and, yes, imitation. Learning to "take off" or "add" seconds is also somewhat instinctive. There are, however, ways in which you can prevent yourself from being greatly over or under the proper time.

First, consider the problem. In the average one-minute spot, there are between 120 and 140 words of dialogue. Look at an average line, count the words in it, then multiply the number of lines. If your answer is 192 words, then you know you really have to move along. If the answer is 84, you know you have a leisurely spot, and you can take your time. (This is not always true. Much of the spot could be filled with musical or sound effects, leaving you with 84 words to be said in only 34 seconds, the 24 other seconds being taken up by the music or effects.)

One good way to be sure you are coming in on time is to divide the commercial into four segments. Look at it as if were an oblong-shaped pie. Cut the pie into four horizontal parts. When you reach your first-quarter mark, you should be at 14½ seconds; at the halfway point, you should be at 29; at the three-quarter mark, your watch should say 42¾.

To check your time accurately you should have a stopwatch (a sweep dial on an ordinary watch is helpful but is not a real substitute). Many pros have a stopwatch wristwatch. A regular stopwatch which you can place on the table alongside your script is preferable. When you reach your mark consult your script to see if you should speed up or slow down.

If you are behind, don't speed up suddenly. Gradually increase your speed so that it is scarcely noticeable. Then look again at the halfway mark. If you're still behind, increase the speed some more—if ahead, slow down a little. Remember, no sudden changes of speed.

The best place to take out excess time is in the pauses. Shorten each pause a little. That way, the dialogue is still clear, and the performance will sound substantially the same and be shorter.

In duo or trio performances, a lot of time often is lost by missing cues—even by as little as a quarter or an eighth of a second. Being slow in your response breaks the rhythm of the performance and makes it sound amateurish.

Miking on Camera

Varying positions from the mike can achieve different effects, but when working on camera, the mike is in a fixed position and we cannot vary our distance from it. Here are some ways you might be miked on camera:

The mike is in a fixed position over your head, out of view of the lens.

The mike is on a movable boom that follows your moves and can be turned by the boom operator to pick up your voice to best advantage.

A lavalier mike is worn around your neck and is hidden in your clothing. A cable extends from the mike to the control room. This allows you freedom of movement, but you are on a leash, and if you must leave the set, the engineer must disengage the cable so you can walk out carrying part of the cable—your "train."

You might wear a lapel mike. It is similar to the lavalier mike in that a cable connects with the control room. It is a smaller mike than the lavalier mike and is used for some talk shows and weather shows. It is seldom used for commercials because it is in view of the camera.

Body miking often is used in shooting outside, where the camera has a broad range of view and where it would be difficult to hide the mike. Here a mike is secreted in the neck area, and a wire goes from the mike to a small transmitter in the small of the back. The transmitter then transmits to a receiver and recorder out of sight of the camera. However, many times when recording out doors, the mike picks up extraneous sounds that seriously interfere with the recorded voice. When that happens, the actor must go to a sound studio, where he can see the film of his performance and hear it at the same time. He then "lip syncs" or "dubs" the commercial to match the lip movement of the filmed commercial.

The Reel Thing

or

A "How-to" for Your Voice-Over Demo Tape

Don Kobiela

Mr. Kobiela is one of TV's most successful voice-over announcers and an instructor of the voice-over course at the Weist-Barron School in New York. You've heard him on hundreds of radio and TV commercials.

Sometimes, instead of a live audition, you may be asked to submit a tape with a sample of your voice-over work. This is called a demo tape (demonstration tape).

In the broadcast business your demo tape is your calling card, résumé, and personal marketing strategy all rolled into one. It's what gets you through agents' doors, into casting directors' offices, and subsequently into your banker's good graces. It had better be the best you have to offer!

I generally recommend that a reel consist of anywhere from six to ten spots, encompassing every type of commercial that you do well. Show off your "soft read," your "hard sell," your sensual, your friendly, your intimate, etc. Similar-sounding spots, however, should not be placed next to one another. A "soft sell," for example, works much more effectively when preceded by a supermarket spot and followed by a "just folks" type. It's framed. And it in turn frames its neighbors, adding variety.

Obviously, your best foot should step forward first, so place what you consider your best spot at the head of the reel, and keeping in mind contrasting juxtaposition, follow with your next best, etc. I've found it effective to end the reel with a character voice, or at least a "character type" voice. Your reel then says, "Hey, I can do this sell, and that sell . . . and oh, yeah, P.S., I also can do something else." So, you ask, where do I get those commercials to put on a demo reel? If you've ever recorded any commercials in real life, so much the better. If not, then you'll have to collect copy, and practice, and then spend some time and dollars at your friendly neighborhood recording studio. (You can pick up copy—and make good connections at the same time—from the folks at the local studios, and from TV and radio stations. Or you can simply record it off the air and transcribe it for yourself.)

OK, you've done all that and you've put together a bundle of spots on tape. That's it, right?

Not quite!

I was at an agent's office once when she was listening to a pile of demo tapes. She'd listen to a bit of a tape—the first spot—then fast-forward her tape recorder to the next, and so on. The part of the tape she heard was determined strictly by luck. For all I know, she may have heard the absolute worst!

The point here is simple: Edit down the spots you've chosen so that they run about 15 to 20 seconds (or even shorter). *You* choose the portion of the spot that will be heard; then the agent can't play "tape Russian roulette" with your reel.

Some final notes: Don't overproduce any demo spot you record. Yes, you should have a music track laid down behind the audio track, but some sound engineers get carried away with their job and select music and sound effects that completely overpower the voice track. Remember, *you* are supposed to be showcased, *not* the production techniques. On the other hand, don't just lay down voice tracks. It sounds amateurish. If a jingle is used, drop all except a few seconds of it.

Similarly, don't overproduce your introduction on the tape. If you wish, just your name at the head of the tape will do fine. (A fancy-schmancy production intro might be OK for local markets, but not in New York, Chicago, and L.A., where casting folks and agents just don't have the time to listen.)

Don't pass around a plain white box demo reel. The five-inch tape reel (at 7½ inches per second) is the standard of the industry, but make sure you add something to the box itself. The packaging is the first thing that meets the eye, even before your voice meets the ear, so if the agent or casting director is impressed with your cover, he or she is set up to be impressed by what's inside.

Do I need a cassette as well as my five-inch reel? Some actors carry a cassette recorder-player so they can give an on-the-spot demonstration of their talents. As for me, in the past five years I've been asked for a cassette of my demo reel only twice.

Anyhow . . . good luck and good voice!

Voice-overs in New York

You hear a disembodied voice coming from the tube. It sounds familiar, but you can't quite place it. Well, let's help you out. Does it sound like José Ferrer? David Wayne? Maybe Burgess Meredith? (You may get that one. He played the Penguin in the *Batman* TV series and the fight trainer in *Rocky* and *Rocky 2*.) Or Orson Welles? (You really have a tin ear if you can't identify that voice!) These are but a few of the well-known actors who specialize in doing voice-overs for national commercials.

If these actors are so famous, why does the sponsor not take advantage of their name value? Why not insert a line in the copy saying, "This is David Wayne for American Airlines"? There are three good reasons. First, the sponsor is selling his product, not the actor. Second, in twenty-eight seconds of copy (the length of a thirty-second commercial), there isn't time for a name announcement, and third (and this is the most important reason) the actor *does not want his name used.* The actor wants to preserve a certain amount of anonymity. Oh, yes, you may recognize the voice, but if the name were used every time, sponsors might well get tired of hearing the actor's name so often and seek another spokesperson.

Ever hear of Peter Thomas, Mason Adams, Bob Kaliban, Alex Scourby, or Don Kobiela? The chances are they are completely unknown to you, but you've heard their voices literally hundreds of times. These and many others are the highly trained announcers whose services are constantly in demand. Although all of them are capable of delivering a variety of approaches to the copy, it is generally their *style* that is their trademark and is sought after by the sponsors.

The great majority of these pros rarely appear on camera. They, like the stars, want to preserve their anonymity. They have no wish to be overexposed, to have the sponsors get tired of them. There is another reason for their wanting to show only their voice, not their face. Many times in a campaign the client will shoot a number of spots. There may be one on-camera spokesperson in all of the spots, and if so, he or she generally works exclusively with that client and cannot work on camera for any other. In the majority of campaigns, however, different actors are used in each spot, while the same voice-over announcer is used in all. Although the fee is slightly less for the voice-over announcer, the usage adds up to more money.

At this point you might well ask, "With so many stars and pros already in the field, what chance is there for me?" Well, just as these announcers for commercials are in demand because of their distinctive voices and styles, so could *you* be. As mentioned earlier, you don't have to have "well-rounded tones." Meredith's voice is certainly not as mellifluous as Ferrer's. There was a time when Ralph Bell (he of the gravelly voice) couldn't get arrested as an announcer; now he's one of the busiest in the business. His voice and style are distinctive . . . they're strictly his own, but if it is purity of enunciation and tone you're looking for, you seek out Alex Scourby. And so it goes.

There are two categories of voice-over spokespeople: straight voice and character voice. Seldom do the twain meet in one announcer. It is not that the "straight" announcers are incapable of doing character voices (Bob Kaliban has a repertory of comic voices that can roll you on the floor with laughter), it is just that they have made their fame in the "straight" department and so are called for that kind of announcing. Likewise, the character people seldom cross over into the straight announcing field.

What do we mean by character voices? Accents, like the "down Maine" New England accent that Parker Fennelly made famous when he was selling Pepperidge Farm products. Screwy voices, like the Keebler Elves, or Charley the Tuna. And let's not omit the distaff side. Hedy Galen and Ruth Franklin each have a gallery of voices ranging from those of newborn infants to tottering great-grandmothers. And how would you like to bank the check the Jolly Green Giant gets just from going, "Ho, ho, ho"?

If you have been an habitual "life of the party" and have wowed assembled guests with your accents and your stories, if you have fooled around doing "impressions," perhaps you can put your talent to work. You will need a professional demo tape just like the one described in the preceding pages. Record your best accents and most distinctive voices, making them all ten to fifteen seconds, or shorter.

Hollywood is the home of the animated cartoon. A few well-known creators of "cartoon voices" do most of the work, but with new cartoons always being filmed, if you are *very* good you might make a stab at it. As with all the other work in Hollywood, in most instances you will need an agent to represent you.

So get going, you with the funny voice (or voices). The laughs you got in a local pub over a few beers may buy you champagne someday.

Recording Radio Commercials

Radio commercials are usually made in an audio studio that has no film facilities, or even in a studio at your local radio station. The procedure is very similar to doing a voice-over for TV. Stand ten to twelve inches from the mike. At this distance you can talk directly into it. If you have to move close, remember you must now talk *across* the mike. The engineer will ask you for a level. Read until told to stop. It takes time for the engineer to adjust his dials to get the best sound from you. So don't just read a single line and then stop.

Your cue to start will be given to you by the engineer through the "talk-back" from the control room. Your timing technique will now stand you in good stead, even more than it did for TV commercials. The reason? There are very few sixty-second TV commercials made, but many radio commercials run a full minute.

If you are late for your recording date (which you should not be, of course), don't rush into the studio saying, "I'm sorry I'm late, but I'm all ready to go." Unfortunately, you are not. If you have been rushing and out of breath, take a few minutes at least to calm down and "get your breath." If your diaphragm and lungs are not relaxed, you will probably run out of breath before you finish a sixty-second commercial.

Radio commercials sometimes require a "harder sell' then on-camera commercials. "Hard sell" means more voice and stronger emphasis. "Soft sell" is just the opposite—reduce the volume and be careful not to overemphasize.

Film Narration

"Narration" is the term applied to making a voice track to be used with an industrial or educational film. It may be done in a studio such as the one described in the section on radio commercials, using a footage counter, or it may be done "wild"—recorded in small segments with spaces left in between so the film editor or "cutter" can later synchronize the recorded track with the film—"lay in" the voice track, as it sometimes is termed.

Narration is really storytelling, not selling. Reading rules apply as far as color, transition, and inflection are concerned, but emphasis is considerably toned down. Since the narration could be as much as thirty minutes long, or even longer, pay a great deal of attention to changes of pitch, pace, and mood. Your narration must have variety throughout or you will sound repetitious and deadly.

Many times you will be able to get a copy of the script in advance of the recording, which will give you a chance to practice it. Often you will find technical terms that might give you difficulty, so it is good policy to ask that difficult words be spelled out phonetically on a separate sheet, so you can become very fluent in their pronunciation by the time you arrive for the recording.

Be sure you really understand what you are saying; don't just plow ahead with your reading. Mark obscure passages and have them explained to you before you rehearse in the studio.

Record the script into a cassette and play it back until you really like the sound. Do you hear enough variety? Is there a smoothness, a flow to your delivery? Or does it sound choppy? The better prepared you are, the more professional you will sound on your first read-through in the studio.

Announcers

For those interested in being announcers, it's a tough market. Fewer are used every year. For your information, however, here is an actual memo for prospective announcers. The memo was written by a network some years ago, when announcers were invariably men, but it applies to women as well.

TV Stations employ only thoroughly experienced announcers—men who have attained a high degree of professional competence. Network announcing is so exacting in its requirements that it can be entrusted only to experienced men [or, now, women]. They do not maintain a school for announcers and have no facilities for apprentice training in this field. Neither courses of instruction nor apprenticeship can take the place of experience in preparing a man for network announcing.

Minimum requirements for an announcer's audition at our networks in New York are five years experience on the staff of one or more large commercial radio or television stations and a B.A. degree, or its equivalent. If you have these qualifications, a live audition will be arranged.

It is possible for an announcer to become proficient in less than the minimum required by us. From long experience with announcers, however, we have found that few can absorb enough broadcasting know-how to be of genuine value to the network in less than that time. At a local station an announcer—experienced or inexperienced—rarely becomes an asset in less than six months; many announcers need more time to learn the policies and practices of the station. Until an announcer is thoroughly schooled in "station" broadcasting, it is not logical to expect him to become familiar with the more complex problems of "network" broadcasting—problems often similar to those of the individual station, but magnified many times.

Since we employ a single announcing staff for both radio and television, we look for certain television qualifications only after we have satisfied ourselves that a candidate is a top-flight radio announcer. After all, most of the announcer's work in television is off-camera. Basically, he must present a pleasant, well-groomed appearance, though not necessarily handsome. He must have poise and self-assurance—an unstudied manner. We do not look for any particular "type" of appearance, because television allows for a wide range of visual personalities.

In every audition, an effort is made to judge the announcer's feeling for pace, for timing, for variety and imaginative interpretation within the limits of idiom and reason. Considerable time is spent with each qualified applicant, in discussing individual problems.

An announcer is much more than a voice, though a good voice—properly used—can be an asset. A good "telephone" voice need not necessarily be a good radio voice; many good radio voices register poorly on the telephone. The telephone reproduces a relatively narrow range; hence it favors certain types of voices; super-sensitive radio, on the other hand, reproduces a wide range and is just as apt to accentuate the bad voice qualities as the good. "Announcing" on a public address system or recording device is not a substitute for radio broadcasting experience, though each can provide an opportunity for testing voice characteristics—if equipment of good quality is used.

There is no specific voice requirement for radio and television broadcasting. Voices of all kinds have been successful when their owners have been exceptionally wise, witty, sensible or charming. For announcing, a friendly, well-modulated, masculine voice is a help. Excessive nasal resonance, mouthy quality, reediness, unusual high or low pitch are disadvantages which should be corrected early if possible. Speech defects such as marked lisping, sharp "S" sounds, a thick-tongued quality, are severe handicaps. Stammering and stuttering are probably a bar to a broadcasting career.

The voice itself, then, is not of prime importance. The intelligence of the announcer is the fundamental requisite—general knowledge and the practical ability to make it count—intelligence in the art of communication. Spoken words are a means of communicating ideas and arousing emotions. The manner of utterance is of great importance to broadcasting. By his way of saying words, a good announcer gains attention, holds it, and convinces. The announcer's manner of speech must not stand between the writer and the listener; must not hinder communications; must be acceptable to the listener in his most relaxed surroundings—his home, his car, etc.

An announcer must sound as if he were talking although, as a matter of fact, he is almost always reading aloud from a script. Except where the script requires another interpretation, he should speak as an educated American, familiar with various parts of the country, sincere and natural, a man with something to say worth listening to.

An announcer must not allow the ends of his phrases to be lost in a vanishing cadence nor should he mumble or slur the distinctive sounds of his words. Real speech is often careless. An announcer tries to give the effect of unpretentious ease and simple directness, while he makes every word audible, and rhetorically useful. If he is successful in concealing his art, he sounds "natural." If the listener is conscious of his devices, he fails to convince and may be called a "ham" or worse.

To give the effect of speaking, an announcer should use the phrasing, the cadences, and the voice quality of idiomatic American *speech,* not of song, recitative or sweet crooning. The pattern of everyday speech is extremely subtle. We can say, however, that one way to phrase well is to understand and to deliver the meaning of sentences, without treasuring single words or dwelling upon syllables. (To treasure words as individual pearls, to dwell upon syllables, to listen to the beauty of one's own voice makes sense impossible.)

Words and syllables normally unstressed in speech cannot be stressed in broadcasting without damaging the illusion of "talking" and requiring a special effort of the listener. The listener's ear is attuned to the phrasing, cadences and inflections common to conversational speech. Overstresses, strange inflections and voice acrobatics so distort the acceptable patterns that the meaning is often lost.

Inexperienced men who wish to enter the announcing field will find no easy path. Announcing is a highly specialized and highly competitive profession. Network requirements are more rigid than those of a local station because network announcers are more widely heard. *But local stations have comparable obligations to their own listeners and clients.* They, therefore, prefer to hire experienced announcers. Increased activity in television has undoubtedly provided new positions, but most new stations also need experienced performers. Thus the beginner is confronted at once with the paradoxical problem of needing experience and not having an easy way to get it.

If, in spite of these considerations, you still wish to try announcing, there are two possible paths to follow: first, *you may enroll in any of the schools specializing in radio and television,* or take special courses in any one of many universities and colleges, or, second, you may take a nonannouncing job with a small radio station and hope that you will be able to gravitate, in time, towards announcing.

Specialized courses can be helpful up to a certain point—to provide useful information and some laboratory practice—but far beyond that you must test your training and your fitness *in a commercial broadcasting station.* Reputable schools *will not* promise to make an announcer of you. Academic courses may be taken within regular college curricula, or, in a more abbreviated form, in evening sessions. These courses can at least serve as an aptitude test. At most, they can prepare you for a more professional, less painful audition.

As for the second way, many persons have become announcers after doing other, often unrelated jobs within a radio station. If you have experience in writing, sales, news-gathering or maintenance of technical equipment, or in clerical or secretarial work—such experience sometimes leads to announcing. If you can begin by rendering some such service of immediate value to the station, you may eventually get an opportunity to go on the air. Most important is establishing yourself at the station, gaining the respect and confidence of your employers. Then, starting with comparatively unimportant duties in broadcasts, you may, in a reasonable time, have the opportunity of saying a few words into the microphone. If you are successful, more important assignments will come.

Remember that despite the aura of glamour, broadcasting is a *business.* To expect to become an announcer without training and experience is as unreasonable as hoping to fly without instruction. And among American young men, there is probably more talent for flying than for announcing. Finally, don't be misled by a rumor that all radio and television announcers earn big salaries; the announcers who make fabulous sums are few.

Your degree of determination to excel in an announcing career—along with continued hard work—will go far in attaining your goal in the announcing profession.

Network announcers are currently being "phased out." That means as announcers retire, none are being hired to take their places. However, much of this article is applicable to hiring announcers for local stations. The larger the station, of course, the stricter the requirements.

Reading
Techniques

Good Delivery Can Be Learned

"I read a commerical for my husband and he said it sounded terrible! He told me I'd never be able to do a commercial. After all, he said, 'You're not an actor.' "

He may have been right on the first count, but he was wrong on the second. You *can* learn to do commercials. You can learn to deliver a commercial with the proper emphasis and enthusiasm. You can learn to sell. And you don't have to be an actor to do it.

Many Americans use a very small range of inflections when they speak. Their range may encompass only a few notes on the vocal scale. As a result, their speech is dull and lifeless. You must have heard someone speaking French, Italian, or Spanish. Maybe your reaction was, "What are they so excited about?" Their excitement may have been due in part to the intensity with which they spoke, but another element was the use of a wide range of inflections.

Inflection is but one of the reading techniques we will be discussing in the following pages. Since they are techniques, they are of course "technical" and you may have difficulty absorbing them at first, but this technical approach to reading commercials has proved effective in transforming actors and nonactors into top-notch commercial performers.

The Actor and the Commercial Performer

It certainly is a help to have acting training before embarking on a career in commercials. An actor knows how to read lines intelligently, has had training in memorization, and knows how to project his or her personality—all traits that must be attained by the commercial performer in order to be successful.

The question that comes to mind, then, is why does an actor need to school himself in the art of performing commercials? Can't he just perform as he does on the stage?

To answer those questions let us begin by discussing acting in general. An actor must change the style of his acting to suit his medium. There is stage acting, acting for motion pictures, acting for television (drama and comedy). Then comes acting for commercials. Although all are related and all require acting ability, they each require special techniques.

The stage actor must have sufficient vocal projection to reach the farthest seat in the theater. His facial expressions and gestures must be broad enough to be effective from a distance, and he must be able to memorize many lines of dialogue.

The motion picture actor must tone down his vocal projection and gestures without losing energy and vitality. In close-ups he must be subtle in the use of his eyes and facial expressions. He does not have to retain long pages of dialogue in his memory, because for the most part he is photographed in short scenes (called "takes").

The television soap opera actor must combine stage and motion picture techniques. Since scenes are continuous and not shot in pieces, his memory must be good. When playing in close-ups he must employ the subtleties required of the screen actor. In longer shots his playing can be a little broader, but he must often make a quick change to the subtlety of the close-up. So he must know the shot that is being taken and remember it during the taping.

Essentially the sitcom actor must employ the same techniques as the soap opera actor, but the sitcom actor also must have a good sense of comedy, and he must know to wait for his laughs if the show is taped with a live audience. Both the actor and director have the problem of anticipating where the laughs will come and leaving spaces for them when the laugh track is added.

Now we come to the commercial actor. We might call commercial acting "instant acting." In twenty-eight seconds (the actual length of a thirty-second commercial) or less, a characterization must be projected that retains its "reality" while strongly making the sales points. Whether it is "hard sell" or "soft sell," the sales points must be made with conviction. In watching commercials on TV we may occasionally be reminded of a line spoken to the Queen by Hamlet: "Me thinks the lady doth protest too much." But the commercial actor *is* protesting. He is arguing with only one side of the argument being presented. Think of this while practicing commercials. Think of how strongly you emphasize your points when you are arguing with someone, and incorporate the same emphasis into reading your copy.

In a commercial the stage actor will often make the mistake of simply giving information—*telling* us about the product instead of *selling* the product. He will think of the *sense* of the line instead of the *sell* of the line. To illustrate the difference, let us take a commercial for Aqua Chiffon.

We have been talking about Aqua Chiffon all the way through the commercial. Now we come to the final line: "So get new Aqua Chiffon at your grocer's today." The actor puts the emphasis on the word "get." Logically the actor thinks, "We've mentioned the product five times. By now everyone should know what we're talking about. So now it's time to tell them to buy the product, so I'll emphasize the word 'get.' "

The commercial actor also hits the word "get," but just to make sure the audience remembers the name of the product, he also puts the emphases on the product name. He reads the line: "So GET NEW AQUA CHIFFON at your grocer's today."

In the following pages we will be presenting techniques of reading and the physical presentation of commercials. Method actors may protest that such a "studies" approach is not acting but indicating. Maybe so. But commercials are not theater, they are advertising. Although some commercials may be amusing, the primary aim is not to amuse or entertain, but to sell. There is precious little time to study motivations, develop a character, or "grow into a part." These luxuries are reserved for actors in the other categories of acting. The commercial actor must give an "on the spot" performance.

Now to script analysis and the techniques which, if studied and practiced well, can help you become an effective commercial actor.

But before we begin, purchase an inexpensive cassette recorder so you can listen to what you have done.

Using the Cassette Recorder-Player

By recording and playing back commercials you will be able to check your presentation. Many people, until they have trained themselves, are not really able to hear exactly where they are placing their voice and how they are inflecting it as they are reading. The more you practice with a tape recorder, playing back your readings, the sooner you will tune your ear so that you will know exactly what you have done vocally without a playback—very important when you are auditioning.

You may, of course, get the same benefits when you use a cassette recorder that is part of your stereo set and not portable. The advantage of the portable recorder is that you can carry a prerecorded tape with you when you go to an interview or audition. Sometimes the occasion arises to demonstrate your capability on the spot. "I just happen to have my audition tape with me on a cassette!"

Recording from Radio or TV

You can learn much about effective delivery of commercials by recording them off the air on your tape recorder and playing them back again and again. A single hearing is not enough for you to absorb exactly what the performer is doing. Should you imitate? Yes, at first. It makes you listen closely and makes you use inflections and rhythms that may be new to you and can be incorporated into your own personal style once you have perfected them. All artists must have some model to follow in the beginning of their studies— painters, singers, musicians. The famous violinist Itzhak Perlman says that in his early years he was influenced by all the great violinists that he had heard play or whose recordings he had listened to: Heifetz, Menuhin, Kreisler and many others. No, there is nothing wrong with imitation, and you will find it difficult to imitate exactly unless you are a born mimic.

The best procedure is to record the commercial first, then time it, and then advance the tape for an equivalent time—perhaps a little longer. Record several commercials following the same procedure. Now play back the commercials in order, recording your imitated version in the blank spaces. Repeat the whole process a number of times until you think you have recorded good "imitations."

The next step is take some of the commercial copy in the book and try to read it, giving an imitation of what you have recorded from radio or TV. You will find that you can in no way give a "carbon copy" of the deliveries you have been attempting to imitate, but you will discover new and interesting things in your interpretations.

Don't be disturbed by the quality of the voice you will hear on a small tape recorder. It is impossible to get a very good quality of vocal reproduction using it, because the speaker is so small. You will, however, hear the inflections in your voice accurately. (It is often possible to play back tapes from your cassette recorder through your sound system, which should give you a much better quality of reproduction. When buying a recorder, you might want to purchase one that has an attachment you can plug into your own set.)

When you are practicing in front of a mirror to check your visual performance, turn on your tape recorder to see if your reading remains the same as it was when you were just recording your voice. You may find a drop in energy level, due to the fact that you were concentrating on your physical performance. Remember, all rehearsals should be at performance level, whether at home or in the studio. The habits you form at home will stand you in good stead when you are in the studio.

A Marking System

Many performers develop a system for marking their scripts to help them remember how they have decided to read their copy so that they can read it the same way each time. If they get a suggested change in their reading from the director, they simply revise their markings.

There follow some simple markings that will clue you into how you have prepared your script. Remember, mark only if you know that the script at the audition will be yours alone and will not have to be used by others. You may use some of the markings or all, depending on how easy or how hard it is for you to remember your prepared reading. If you have trouble reading the script the same way each time, the markings relieve the burden of recalling your preparation, so you can concentrate on those other elements in your delivery—enthusiasm, pace, degrees of inflection, etc., that would be hard to indicate by marks.

If you make every mark we have suggested, it will look like a chicken has walked over your script. When you are practicing at home, however, make all the marks at first. This will train you to be conscious of the techniques you are employing. Of course, you may invent your own system, but be consistent. If a circle means "color" one time, it must mean "color" every time, and so forth.

The Marks

Punch: an <u>underline</u> to show the word or words to be emphasized

Color: a (circle) to denote the word to be colored

Inflection: a mark sliding upward to indicate a sliding-upward inflection,   or one sliding down to indicate a downward inflection⌒ (period or false period)

High ending: a short, straight line over the last syllable of the word with a downward slide at the end
                (example: Revlon⌒)

Transition: a half bracket⌐ if you intend to start a transition high, or⌊_ if you intend to start low. The mark should precede the word
                (example: ⌐ Revlon or   ⌊Revlon

Eyes up: a half-bracket close __/at the end of the word when your eyes should be up and looking at the lens
                (example: Revl<u>on</u>/)

Short pause: a single vertical line / For a longer pause, two vertical lines //

If you are ever asked to give an "up reading," it means a "high ending," not a sliding-upward inflection. (See the section on inflections.) A "low ending" may be referred to as a "down reading."

N.B.: When working on the exercises in this section, *do not mark your book*. Make a copy of the exercise and mark the copy.

Script Analysis

Before you begin to employ your reading techniques you must of course thoroughly understand what the script is saying. You must analyze the script.

Commercials, even the worst ones, do not just happen, as we have explained. They are planned, thought about, worked over, fought over, changed, and then finally cast and produced. Have some respect for them! They are not written to amuse—but rather to inform and *sell the merchandise!*

Your job is to discover the correct way to read the commercial.

What is the correct way? Usually, the correct reading most clearly brings out the copywriter's sales message. Most commercials follow a pattern: problem, solution, result.

Because the purpose of a commercial is to sell, they all must contain the kind of points made in any good sales pitch.

The commercial tries to capture the prospect's interest. The initial section is usually an attention-seeking gimmick.

The name of the product for sale is mentioned.

The commercial explains why this product is better than others of the same type—it explains the principal point of difference.

The commercial then tells the listener what the product will do for him—how fine he'll feel—how well his car will run—how nice she will smell.

The commercial asks for the order: "please buy it." It tells you where the product can be obtained and in what sizes.

Each of these sections should be approached in a different mood or style. For example, the first could be folksy, the second prideful, the third explanatory, etc. This change from mood to mood is called a transition or a change of key.

All of the elements are not always present. There may be more sections; there may be fewer. They are not always in the order given here. Now that you know the major sections, read the left (video) side of the script (if there is a video side; some scripts omit it). It tells you who, what, and where you are. This will seriously affect your approach.

Look for the marketing problem. Every advertiser has a sales problem (also known as the marketing problem). What was the problem of Listerine? Of Virginia Slims? Of Goodrich? What problem is shared by S.O.S, Marcal Tissues, and Royal Gelatin? Every commercial shows the particular problem inhibiting the sale of the product and tries to overcome public sales resistance to it.

If you have undertaken the prior steps, the key words and phrases should be evident. Ask yourself:
- What was the aim of the commercial?
- What was the marketing problem?
- What are the most important key words?

The Question-and-Answer Method

If you examine a commercial you will discover that every commercial is just a series of answers to unspoken questions. It is almost as if the copywriter is attempting to answer the questions presumed to be in the minds of the audience. Knowing this can be very helpful to actors; it means that all you need to do is find the proper question that precedes each answer, then answer that question in a natural way, line for line.

There is, however, one catch: For "opening lines" there is seldom a question, so the actor must usually open "on his own," using the float-in method. You can play this question-and-answer game with a friend or someone in your family. Be sure, when you do, however, that you answer the questions (using the exact wording of the text script) every bit as naturally as your questioner asks them. The example below will explain the method more clearly:

Here is a script without any questions inserted:

ANNOUNCER: Good news! Now Digesto comes in six delicious flavors. Raspberry, orange, lemon, lime, strawberry, and chocolate. Now you can get rid of upset stomach fast and enjoy the taste of real fruit flavors. Remember, Digesto comes in six delicious flavors. Look for it at your drugstore—today.

Not very natural dialogue, is it? But it can be made more natural by the insertion of questions. For example:

Good news! [What's the good news?] Now Digesto comes in six delicious flavors. [Yeah? What are they?] Raspberry, orange, lemon, lime, strawberry, and chocolate. [So what?] Now you can get rid of upset stomach fast

[Anything more?] and enjoy the taste of real fruit flavors. [What do you want me to know?] Remember, Digesto comes in six delicious flavors. [What do you want me to do?] Look for it [Where?] at your drugstore [When?]—today.

Four Keys to the Effective Delivery of Commercials

Punch: Emphasizing the words that will give the sentence the correct meaning.
Color: Making words sound like what they mean.
Inflection: The rise and fall of the voice.
Transition: The change of subject, thought, or mood.

Punch

In order to bring out the meaning of a commercial, we must first emphasize the proper words. "Elementary," as Holmes would say to Watson. Yes, but how to find the proper words? If we subtract all the unnecessary words, we will end up with the *root meaning* of the sentence. The dying cowboy would like to say, "I've been shot. Get a posse together and go to Laredo, and find a man named Jackson." But the cowboy hasn't the strength to say all that, so he says, "Shot. Get posse, Laredo. Find Jackson."

Another way to think of determining the root meaning is by imagining that you are writing a telegram. You want to save words, so you use just the words that will convey your meaning.

In the following commercial we have italicized the words that would go into your telegram.

If you could *pour* your *mouthwash* into your *toothpaste* you could *skip* the whole *gargling* bit. *That's* the *idea* behind Colgate's new *Mouthwash Toothpaste. Its concentrated* mouthwash *ingredients,* the *stuff* that *makes* mouthwash *work,* are as *effective* and *last* as *long* as a leading *mouthwash. You want* mouthwash in your *toothpaste?* Colgate's new *Mouthwash Toothpaste* is *for people* who *brush* and *gargle.*

Remember, changing the punch can completely change the meaning of the sentence, as in the sentence, "I didn't say he stole the dog."

> *I* didn't say he stole the dog.
> I *didn't* say he stole the dog.
> I didn't *say* he stole the dog.
> I didn't say *he* stole the dog.
> I didn't say he *stole* the dog.
> I didn't say he stole *the* dog.
> I didn't say he stole the *dog*.

As you punch the underlined word in the above sentence you will discover there are seven different meanings to the very same sentence.

Methods of Punching

1. Increasing the volume of the word to be punched—saying the word a little louder than the other words.
2. Decreasing the volume, sometimes even to a whisper. "I'm sorry to tell you that you have *bad breath*."
3. Raising the word to a higher note in your vocal register. "It's not only *better*, it's the *best!*"
4. Lowering the word in your vocal register. "Excel coffee has a marvelous *aroma*."
5. Gapping—leaving a pause before and after the word to be punched, or just before, or just after. "Painex has not—*one*—but—*two*—pain-killing ingredients."
6. Distorting the word by lengthening a vowel or a consonant. "It is cooold in here." "It was a rrrrough night."

For added emphasis you may combine two punch methods. In example 5 the words "one" and "two" could be "gapped" and "raised" at the same time.

By far the most used method of punching is to raise the word in your vocal register.

At times two words must be punched equally, as in "bad breath," or there may be a whole series of words that require equal emphasis. In the following example note the single, double, and multiple punching.

When *Revel* builds an *eye shadow* she builds it to *last*. *Fifty beautiful young super shadows*, built *step* by *step* for *beautiful, lasting color*. A cream for smoothness, a *natural protein,* a *silky color.* All three *triple-blended together* into Revel's *super shadows* for a *dynamite look* that's built to *last.*

Punch Exercises

In the following commercials, underline the single, double, and multiple punching, then check the "answers" (p. 143) for proper markings. (Remember, do not underline in your book. Copy or photocopy the exercise and underline the copy.)

Always thought noodles were all the same? Well, the next time you're in the market, take a peek in the window of a package of Ratazzi Egg Noodles. Here's what you'll see. Golden noodles! Rich, golden noodles—the color of the yolks of country-fresh eggs. And that's exactly where Ratazzi Egg Noodles get their color. They're made with golden yolks. Only egg yolks! And when you lift Ratazzi Egg Noodles out of the cooking pot, pile 'em on a platter, drizzle 'em with butter—you'll find they're the tenderest noodles, the lightest, tastiest noodles you've ever eaten. Ratazzi Egg Noodles. Pay just a little more and you get the best.

Years ago kids were nibblers—and they're still nibblers. Kids haven't changed. But what's in some of the things they're nibbling? That's changed. For the worse. Harmful stabilizers or preservatives have been added. But not to Snappy Jack. It's all natural ingredients. Wholesome, caramel-coated popcorn—nutritious peanuts. 100 percent natural. Nothing artificial. So let 'em nibble. As long as it's Snappy Jack.

Color

Noah Webster said it: "There are many words in our language which were borrowed from the sensible objects, the ideas of which they are designed to express. Such are the *dashing* of waters, the *crackling* of burning faggots, the *hissing* of serpents."

To dramatize your reading and, in a way, emphasize certain words, we "color" them—make them sound like their meaning. There are four ways to do this: Overemphasize vowels or consonants, fit the pace to the word; fit the pitch to the word; use vocal volume.

Take the words "rough" and "smooth." If we stretch out the "r" in "rough" and shorten the final "gh" ("f"sound) we get "rrrruf," which makes a sound like the meaning of the word. Now "smooth." Prolong the vowel sound (smooth) and slightly reduce your vocal volume.

In other words, speak the word a little more softly than the surrounding words.

Now pace: Say the words "quick as a flash" slowly, stretching out the words. Does it convey the meaning? Now speed up the entire phrase. The phrase now has the proper color.

Vocal pitch: Take the word "aroma." Try it high in your vocal register. Does it sound like an enticing odor? Now drop it in vocal pitch and give full value to the "o" sound. If the word applies to "coffee" in your copy, you can almost smell the coffee.

"Sparkling ginger ale." First try it low in your voice range. Now say it high in your vocal range, pulling back the lips a bit to let all the high resonance emerge. Don't the words sound effervescent?

Vocal volume: Say the word "soft" loudly. Now cut the volume way down. Sound more like it?

How much should you overemphasize or underemphasize words using the above techniques? Your sense of drama, your good taste, your sense of word values must judge. As a general rule: When you color words, don't overdo.

Circle the color words in your script to make them stand out.

When reading a food or beverage commercial a director may say, "Give me more taste appeal." He wants you to color such words as "tasty" or "delicious" to make them sound appetizing.

Now, here is a tempting sight! Delicious, deep-purple Concord grapes. And you can enjoy all their deep-purple goodness when you drink refreshingly wonderful Grape Ade."

Here are some other examples of color words in scripts:

The sky was bright—the sun burning hot. I got a bad burn. But Onextime saved the day. It cooled and soothed my skin.

Fresh. Natural. Real. Today's kind of sexy. The look you get with Glamour Girl make-up. Made with clean, pure ingredients, it makes you feel good about your skin. You feel clean. And today clean is sexy.

Exercise

Circle the color words in the following commercials on a copy of the page, then check your markings in the "answer" section (p. 143).

Sooner or later you'll try one of our White Eagle cigars, and when you do, we're gonna getcha! Maybe with our mild aroma—maybe with our sweet taste. But we're gonna getcha. Real good.

Bott puts the taste of luscious, sun-drenched Florida oranges in new Bott Orange Soda. Mouth-watering Concord grapes in new Grape Soda. Ripe, juicy raspberries in new Bott Raspberry Soda.

Inflection

Inflection can be the most important of the four keys to the effective delivery of commercials. The proper use of inflection helps us to delineate our meaning more accurately and create variety. Improper handling of inflection can make the performer sound bored and unnatural, even though he or she may employ all the other reading techniques correctly.

The performer must learn by inflection how to convert the written text into the spoken text. Sounds easy, doesn't it? The trouble is that most of us when we read aloud sound as if we were reading, not talking to someone. Add to that the element of "sell" that must be present in every commercial presentation, and the fact that the performer must be able to remember exactly what he has done so he can repeat it without change if told to do so, and it becomes evident that just "winging" the copy is not enough. The actor must be made aware of inflection techniques. We say "aware," because many performers instinctively use some of the techniques we will discuss just because they sound right, and are not aware that a technique is involved. Once they understand the reasons for the inflections they are using, they are in command of the copy. Depending just on your instincts can be dangerous, because your instincts may not always be right.

There are three inflections: one that slides upward (rising), one that slides downward (falling), and one that does not change in pitch (constant), produced by sustaining a vowel sound. A famous voice teacher once said, "It is amazing to realize that from only three inflections all the languages and dialects of the world are formed."

Basically the rising inflection denotes incompletion, while the falling inflection denotes completion. The sustaining of a vowel sound is seldom used, and even then at the end of the sound our voice may rise or fall.

When we use a rising inflection in the same register in which we are speaking, it can indicate (1) a question, (2) a series ("apples, peaches, pears, bananas"), (3) a relationship between two words ("black" and "white", "good" or "bad"), or that (4) a second clause must follow to complete the meaning of the first clause ("Because I made a commercial, I now have some money").

Sometimes a director may tell you to deemphasize words that relate to competitive products. Here is an example: "I could give my son one of those chocolate powders or syrups. Instead I give him chocolate-flavored Ovaltine." In a usual reading of the line we are giving as much emphasis to the "powders and syrups" as we are to Ovaltine. To minimize "powders and syrups" we drop the words in our vocal register and end each one with an exaggerated rising inflection. Now it makes our competitor's products sound positively "icky" and we wouldn't give them to the poor boy. We have produced a vocal sneer. Try it and you'll see what we mean.

The falling inflection indicates finality. The degree of finality depends on where the slide starts in our vocal register. If the downward slide starts in our lower register, it indicates we have concluded a subject or ended a commercial. If the slide starts in our higher register, it indicates that although a thought has been completed, there is more to come on the same subject. To put it another way, the falling inflection in our lower register indicates conclusion in our upper register continuance. To differentiate between the two downward slides, we call the higher one a *high ending* and the lower one a *low ending*.

To demonstrate this read the following sentence two ways: "I went to the door and I opened it." The first time end the sentence in your lower register. The second time, place the words "opened it" in your higher register. You will see that the first reading was just a statement of fact, but with the second reading (that has the high ending) we want to know what happened when you opened the door.

A common fault of inexperienced performers is to make every period they see a low ending, with the result that the commercial seems to come to a conclusion after every sentence. It has the effect of making the reader seem bored or disinterested in the copy. A good rule to follow is to keep making high endings until you come to the end of a subject. At that point make a low ending and you are preparing the way for a transition into the next subject, which will be discussed under Transition.

How to Read the Way We Talk

Now let's consider written punctuation versus vocal punctuation. If copywriters would always punctuate the way we speak, it would all be very simple, but this does not occur very often. A sentence may consist of several clauses, may include prepositional phrases and infinitives, and may run on for several lines. Our early training in reading aloud causes many of us to keep all of our inflections rising until we come to the end of the sentence. Then we drop our voice, using a falling inflection to indicate the period. The listener becomes aware that we are reading instead of talking to him, because we don't talk that way.

You see, when we are talking we usually are not aware of how we are inflecting. Our voices may slide down a number of times before we come to the end of the sentence. It is the problem of the reader to analyze each sentence to determine where the inflections would occur if he were speaking.

And how is this determination made? Well, many sentences begin with a simple thought which may not be more than a subject and a verb, and then the thought is amplified by adding prepositional phrases, adverbial phrases, infinitives, or another clause. As an example, let us take a complete thought composed of two words: "Jesus wept"—the shortest verse in the Bible, a simple sentence. At the end of our thought, our voice slides down, making a vocal period.

We've said the verse. Now we remember where the action occurred, so we pause and say, as an afterthought, "—in the garden of Gethsemane." And we make another vocal period after "Gethsemane." Now we remember something else, and we add one more afterthought: "—after the Last Supper." Now another afterthought: "—just before Peter's denial."

You'll observe that our original thought has been amplified by three prepositional phrases, and at the end of each prepositional phrase we have made a vocal period. The sentence now ends with the word "denial," where we place a grammatical period. Since the vocal periods we made after the word "wept" and the prepositional phrases are not grammatical periods, we call them "false periods." Or to put it another way, a vocal period that does not coincide with a grammatical period is called a false period.

Our original thought with its amplifications could be written this way: "Jesus wept. In the Garden of Gethsemane. After the Last Supper. Just before Peter's denial." Now our thought can be delivered the way we talk. Although it is not grammatically correct, it is now vocally correct. In the delivery of the line, however, we ignore the pauses we made for the afterthoughts, since a pause is not required for a false period. In effect we have pulled the sentence together.

In delivering this amplified thought the reader sometimes faces a psychological problem. He knows that the proper sentence does not end until "denial," so even with the vocal periods written in, he substitutes sliding-upward inflections for the false periods. As a result, he now sounds as if he were reading instead of talking to someone. Read the sentence aloud and put sliding-upward inflections at each vocal period and you'll immediately see how "read-y" it sounds. It even sounds a bit silly.

Now we add the final element. If we read our amplified thought making each vocal period a "low ending" our sentence sounds choppy. Make all the vocal periods "high endings" and the sentence flows.

Sometimes commercial copy is written inserting the false periods. For example, here is an actual piece of commercial copy. The product name has been changed along with a few minor changes, but it appears essentially as the copywriter wrote it.

Choosing an antiperspirant spray isn't the most important decision you'll ever make. But since you do have to make that decision, you should know about SAFE. Because it's really different. Lots of antiperspirant sprays go on with a messy powder. Compared to SAFE. Which goes on dry. I'm not saying this proves SAFE keeps you drier. But you can prove that to yourself. In the only place that really counts. Under your arms. Try SAFE on one side. And on the other side, try the spray you like best. Whether it's a powder or not. If you're like most people, the SAFE side will be the drier side. But don't take my word for it. Use your own arms. And find out for yourself. Try SAFE on one side. And it'll convince your other side. We're safe in making that statement.*

---

*You will seldom find copy written as this with all the false periods, although you may find some. You will have to determine the rest for yourself. In fact, since copywriters have their own systems of punctuating, you must first examine the copy, use the punctuation that makes the copy read right to you, and then change the punctuation, which if observed, would made you sound "read-y."

An examination of this commercial copy will show you how to locate false periods. You will note that after a thought is complete there occurs a false period. After each amplification of the original thought, another false period is placed in the copy. You will see that you can stop at any of the false periods and the copy makes sense. In determining your false periods look out for conjunctions and prepositions. In front of most of them you can make a false period. If you don't catch all of them, don't worry. Your reading will still sound pretty good.

Also note in the above the commas after the word "decision" (line 2), after "other side" (line 7), and after "most people" (line 8). In each case a rising inflection is called for, because additional information is required to make the thought complete.

Take particular care when product name occurs in the body of the sentence. If at the end of the product name you use a rising inflection instead of a false period, it will tend to take away the emphasis on the product name. If you remember to punch the word, you will almost always put a false period after the product name.

The Billboard

Sometimes a thought is expressed by just a series of words, or a phrase without a verb. This is called a billboard, and it occurs frequently in commercial copy. The word derives from the advertising billboard, where the message is often presented in clipped phrases without using a verb. The billboard presents copy dramatically and also saves words. At the end of the billboard there is always a vocal period. It is true that grammatically the thought is not complete, but the meaning is understood.

The following ad is expressed in a complete sentence: "This week in all the Macy stores throughout the New York area a Great White Sale is taking place." Now the ad written with billboards: "This week. All Macy stores. New York area. Great White Sale." The meaning is clear, the ad is more dramatic, and words are saved—and words are at a premium in video commercial copy.

If in reading a series of billboards the student has the tendency to link them with rising inflections instead of vocal periods, he can correct this by asking a question before each billboard and then answering it with the text. After all, you cannot give an answer with a rising inflection. For example: "When?" This week. "Who?" All Macy stores. "Where?" New York area. "What?" Great White Sale.

You may find a series of billboards written with commas, periods, or exclamation points following them. If commas are used, change them on your copy to false periods. It should help you to remember not to use rising inflections to link the words. For example, "How do you feel?" With commas, "Great, marvelous, terrific, never felt better." With periods, "Great. Marvelous. Terrific. Never felt better."

Inflections in a Series

When reading a series, most beginners instinctively string the words together with rising inflections: for example, "Apples, peaches, pears, bananas." As you read this you see that the repetition of the same inflection gets a little boring. Now read the series using a falling inflection on "peaches." So the series now goes, "Apples, peaches. Pears, bananas." You can use any combination. Use what sounds right to you.

Inflections may be repeated to produce special effects. Since the vocal period or falling inflection used in the billboard is more punchy and dramatic it is often used to build emphasis, as in the Macy ad above, or to make something sound exciting. On the other hand, if we want to make something sound dull and boring, we can repeat the rising inflection. By elongating and exaggerating the upward slide we emphasize the tediousness we wish to convey. For example: "I worked and worked and slaved and slaved and still didn't get the job done."

As a general rule, use billboards for dramatic words or phrases, and the rising inflection for words that express softness, ease, or relaxation. "Are your hands red. Rough. Harsh to the touch? Would you like them to be soft, smooth, and beautiful?"

As the student begins to apply inflection techniques to his reading, he will find that no commercial is just a lot of dull copy. Each commercial is a separate challenge.

Inflection—Examples

"Saturn, the ultimate personal car, from Chrysler." If you use a rising inflection on "Saturn" you weaken the name of our product. If "car" has a rising inflection, it associates our car with Chrysler. OK.

But now put a false period after "Saturn." The name stands out. Now a false period after "car." So now we have "Saturn. The ultimate personal car. From Chrysler." The meaning is now broadened. Saturn becomes the ultimate personal car of *all* the cars that are made. What a difference in meaning!

"A great-tasting ketchup, and a tomato paste thick and rich with flavor." This line has two distinctly different meanings, depending on the vocal punctuation. (1) "A great-tasting ketchup, and a tomato paste. Thick and rich with flavor." With a rising inflection on "ketchup" and a false period after "paste," "ketchup" and "tomato paste" are joined together in a double billboard, making them both "thick and rich with flavor." (2) "A great-tasting ketchup. And a tomato paste thick and rich with flavor." With a false period after "ketchup," now only the tomato paste is "thick and rich with flavor."

NOTE: In the following exercises do not write your answers in this book. Make a copy and mark that instead, then check your markings in the "answer" section (pp. 143–144).

Inflection Exercise No. 1

Put false periods in the following copy:

Grand National Bank works with this country's leading companies all along the food-production chain to help provide food for consumers in every state in the Union, countries all around the world.

Inflection Exercise No. 2

Mark the rising inflections and false periods in the following commercial:

These are the hands that wash the baby, the hands that soak the diapers, scrub the crib, wash the dress. Baby looks beautiful, but look at those hands—red, rough, harsh to the touch. Hands like these need medicated Lotiana, the hardworking cream for hands that work hard. Lotiana not only softens and smooths, but actually helps heal as no ordinary lotion can—works so fast you can almost feel it start to heal, and you'll see your hands look softer, smoother, lovelier overnight. Remember, a woman's hand have to be soft and smooth for so many reasons. Keep yours looking their loveliest with Lotiana skin cream, the hardworking cream for hands that work hard.

Transition

I'm sure that almost everyone has had the following experience. You're dressing for work in the morning and at the same time listening to the news on the radio—not giving it your full attention. The newscaster is reporting a local fire and then all of a sudden that fire seems to have happened in another city. You're confused. The problem is that the newscaster did not make a vocal change to call your attention to the fact that he was now reporting a different fire; he did not make a good transition.

When you are reading commercials you must make your changes of subject apparent to the listener. You must make effective transitions.

When people are speaking, they change the "mood" or "key" of their voices whenever they change the subject. It is called "a change of attitude" or "a change of perspective." In addition, when the speaker ends a subject, the tone of his voice usually goes lower or higher in his vocal register—he makes a "low ending" or a "high ending." To start the next subject he reverses the pitch—if he ended low, he starts high, or vice versa. This indication to the listener that the subject has been changed is called a "transition."

To strengthen the transition, two things should be added—a change of "pace" and a change of "pattern." To change the pace, you slow down a bit as you end a subject, and you begin the next subject a little faster. Or you may reverse this—end faster, start slower. The contrast in pace makes the transition more apparent to the listener.

To change the "pattern" of your speech you change the way your inflections rise and fall. If you have ever seen an electrocardiogram, you will have observed that with a steady heartbeat, a pattern is drawn on a moving scroll that keeps repeating itself. If such a scroll could give you a visual picture of your speech, you would see how your inflections rise and fall. If the pattern were the same for the second subject as it was for the first, you would not have made a strong transition. If you have access to a cassette recorder you can check your speech patterns audibly by using the "Da-da" method. Simply substitute "da" for every syllable in the script, but read the copy with the same inflections you would give the actual words. The result will sound weird, but you will discover that when the words have been eliminated, your inflections, or "patterns," stand out clearly.

Transitions may occur very frequently in commercials, sometimes between sentences, sometimes even within a sentence. Your signposts within sentences are the conjunctions or phrases that indicate contrast, such as "but," "or," "however," and "on the other hand."

To sum up, the four changes in making a transition are: change of perspective (mood, attitude); change of pitch; change of pace; change of pattern.

The rule for change of pitch and pace is:

End in lower register—slow down, then start in higher register—speed up or

End in lower register—speed up, then start in higher register—slow down.

Or, as indicated above, the rule may be reversed:

End in higher register—speed up, then start in lower register—slow down, etc.

The aim of the transition, of course, is to produce contrast. Any one of the "changes" will help the transition. The more "changes" you can employ, the stronger the contrast, and thus the stronger the transition.

In addition to vocal changes, you should make physical changes to indicate a transition:

A slight change in head position: Lower the head slightly; turn the head a little to one side; cock the head a little to one side.

A brief pause as you shift the head. All changes of head position should be very subtle and the pause very brief, just the normal pause you would take for a period or a comma.

The mark to indicate the transition is a half bracket, thus: if you start high, or   if you start low.

The following is an example of how a commercial you are to audition might appear (transition marks have been added). The left-hand side (video) outlines in brief how the commercial is to be shot. It gives you an idea of the action involved and often can be helpful in your preparation of the copy. In actual practice you will seldom be given a script that contains the video side. Note that some of the spaces coincide with your transitions.

SUDZ (60 seconds)

VIDEO

OPEN ON MCU OF ATTRACTIVE WOMAN IN COTTON HOUSEDRESS IN LIMBO—PICKING UP BOX OF SUDZ OFF TABLE BESIDE HER.

Now!—by popular demand . . .

MOVE IN OR CUT TO CU OF HER FINGER POINTING TO FLATWARE OFFER ON BOX.

WOMAN: (ON—THEN OVER) . . . in every box of new SUDZ—the all-purpose detergent . . .

CUT TO VERY TIGHT CU OF ONE PLACE SETTING (TO SHOW PATTERN) ON DINING-ROOM TABLE. STAINLESS STEEL FLATWARE, CRYSTAL, AND LINEN IN SYNC WITH "STAINLESS." SUPER OVER: "STAINLESS STEEL BY ONEIDA."

. . . handsome stainless-steel flatware by Oneida—in the lovely "Capri" pattern. Women all over the country are telling us how much they like this beautiful stainless-steel flatware in SUDZ.

CUT TO CU OF TOP OF TABLE AS HER HAND TAKES KNIFE FROM THE GIANT-SIZE BOX AND PUTS IT DOWN NEXT TO FORK, THE SOUP/DESSERT SPOON, AND THE SALAD FORK, WHICH ARE FANNED OUT THERE. SHE INDICATES EACH IN SYNC. THEN SHE TAKES TEASPOON OUT OF REGULAR BOX AND LAYS IT DOWN.

Inside the giant-size box, you'll find a knife, or a fork, or a soup/dessert spoon, or a salad fork. And inside the regular-size box, you'll find a teaspoon.

CUT TO CU OF SMARTLY SET TABLE WITH CHINAWARE PROMINENT. (CHINAWARE COMMERCIAL FOOTAGE)

And if you're one of the many women who have been collecting "Wild Rose" pattern chinaware in Sudz . . .

CUT BACK TO WOMAN POINTING TO DIRECTIONS ABOUT CHINAWARE ON BACK OF SUDZ BOX.

WOMAN (ON) . . . here's good news! You can complete your set of "Wild Rose" chinaware quickly and easily by following the simple directions on the back of each new Sudz package.

CUT TO TIGHT CU OF SUDZ BOXES IN LIMBO AND SUPER LEVER GUARANTEE

Start your collection of stainless-steel flatware by Oneida with new Sudz—today! And remember, you can complete your set of chinaware at once!

Example of Transitions

The opening paragraph is all billboards, which calls for punching many words, so you will produce a "punch" pattern. Voice placement in your medium range.

Now! By popular demand! In every box of new Sudz—the all-purpose detergent—handsome stainless-steel flatware by Oneida—in the lovely "Capri" pattern.

Now start higher, talk faster, and roll the words along, not hitting them as hard as in the first paragraph. Your attitude should be one of pride.

Women all over the country are telling us how much they like this beautiful stainless-steel flatware in Sudz. [Start lower and slow down; your attitude—explanatory.] Inside the giant-size box, you'll find a knife, or a fork, or a soup/dessert spoon, or a salad fork. And inside the regular-size box, you'll find a teaspoon! [Slow down and go down as you end, then start higher and faster.] And if you're one of the many women who have been collecting "Wild Rose" pattern chinaware in Sudz, here's good news! [End high and start lower and slower.] You can complete your set of "Wild Rose" chinaware quickly and easily by following the simple directions on the back of each box of new Sudz package. [End lower and slow down just a bit—start higher and faster.] Start your collection of stainless-steel flatware by Oneida with new Sudz—today! And remember, you can complete your set of chinaware at once!

Make a copy of these exercises, then mark your transitions on the copy. Do not mark the book. Check your answers on pages 144–145.

Exercise No. 1

I'm a terrible cook, really I am. But do you know, my pies always turn out wonderful! What I'm proudest of is the crust. It's so light and flaky. But I can't take credit for it, because it's Crispit that does it. Every time! Boy, I can remember when the water problem had me stumped—how much to put in? But now with Crispit there's no guesswork, and my pies are always light and flaky. Believe me, I know from experience, Crispit makes pie crust crisp.

Exercise No. 2

For countertops, choose Topcote. Topcote laminated plastic gives you original designs and beautiful permanent colors. It is heat-resistant, safe from acid and water, and greaseproof.

Look at this dream kitchen. Topcote is so easy to keep clean and shiny—just like new, and Topcote is so decorative. This vanity will always be safe from cosmetic stains. This kitchen will be the envy of your neighbors. Throughout your house use Topcote for all your countertops.

The Four Keys—Conclusion

After reading about the four keys to the effective delivery of commercials, your head may be spinning a bit, and you may ask yourself, "Can I remember all that when I go to an audition?" You are not going to disgrace yourself if you forget an inflection here and there. Of course, the more you remember and put into your reading, the more effective you will be. If you practice conscientiously and play back on a cassette recorder you will find that you will so accustom yourself to the techniques that you hardly have to think about them. They will become second nature. Some of you will discover that you have been using the foregoing techniques all along without being conscious of them or identifying them. If that is the case, the realization that you have been reading effectively should strengthen your self-confidence.

There is another reason why, even if you have been using the foregoing techniques, you should know exactly what you are doing and be able to remember it. As we have said earlier, you may "wing" a commercial, giving a great reading because your instincts are good. Now the director asks you to read the commercial a second time. Without realizing it, you make a small change, and the director says, "That's not how you read the copy the first time." What are you going to say? "How *did* I read it?"

It is the mark of a "pro" to be able to remember exactly how a line was delivered so that it can be repeated again and again without a change unless the director asks for a change. When you are consciously using the four keys to the effective delivery of commercials, you, too, will be considered a pro.

Another question sometimes arises: "If I use all those techniques, am I going to sound natural?" Maybe not to yourself, until you have incorporated the techniques into your own style; but remember, your present "natural style" may be very dull indeed. You may speak in almost a monotone, never using a proper range of inflections. You may give so little emphasis that you sound uninterested in what you are saying. First tape a commercial on a cassette recorder in what you consider your "normal" delivery. Then follow with a recording of the same commercial using the four keys. Now ask a second party to listen to both commercials and tell you which sounds better. Nine times out of ten it will be the second reading, and you may be amazed to hear that your second reading was judged to be the more "natural."

It may be disconcerting at first to hear yourself employing the four keys techniques when formerly your reading was dull and flat. It may actually scare you a bit to find yourself using all those techniques. You're almost like a little puppy who barks for the first time and so frightens himself when he hears his own bark that he runs and hides.

At the back of this book you will find commercials to practice. If you intend to mark the commercials, copy or photocopy the page. Do not mark the book.

Take a deep breath

But you still aren't home free. You have a lot more to learn before you can deliver an effective commercial.

Spokesperson Techniques

The art of the commercial actor is persuasion. There are as many techniques of persuasion as there are facial expressions, gestures, and vocal utterances. But, fortunately, we don't have to learn them all to read commercials well.

We can take consolation in the fact that commercials have a sameness about them, if only because they are all selling something.

Unfortunately, actors in commercial auditions often make the worst possible mistake: They don't study the commercial sufficiently while waiting their turn to read.

What should you be looking for when you study a commercial? It seems that there are three basic questions to be asked about the commercial that, when answered, will supply most of what you need to know:

- Whom are you portraying?
- Whom are you addressing?
- What kind of product are you selling?

There is no order in which these questions should be asked. The answer to one will help supply the answer to another.

With that behind us, we can go on to improve our vocal variety, pauses, false periods, billboards, transitions, etc. . . . . Remember??? Our proficiency in these techniques will enable us to communicate the information we've learned from studying the commercial in the best of all possible ways.

One more hint may help, and it has to do with that first question: "Whom are you portraying?" It seems that there are three main categories into which spokespersons fall. We call these categories "Points of Authority." An agent has sent you on to audition for, in this case, a spokesperson or testimonial commercial. Why? Well, probably because you're the right type. But why would you be an authority on this product? Don't ask the agent. He hasn't seen the copy. Try plugging yourself into one of these categories:

- You're an employee of the company that makes the product. You know how carefully it's made. You know something about the research that went into its creation. You're aware of the care that goes into customer service. You're an authority because you've been involved firsthand, one way or another.
- You're a person who has discovered the product for your own use. You used to use an inferior product, but then you found out about this one. You're a discriminating consumer, and you find this product to be the best of its kind. You understand the needs of the person you're addressing because you've experienced the same needs. You're just like him or her.
- Even more egotistically, you're saying that if the listener uses this product, he or she can be like you. You have a certain desirable quality. Maybe you're sexy, continental, kooky, clean-cut, or calm, cool, and collected about life in general. You give

the impression, though you may not say it in so many words, that if this person uses this product, then he or she will miraculously embody all of your best qualities. Isn't that ridiculous? It works!

Tag Lines

The final line of a commercial (known as the "tag line") is very important. You should be able to do tags several ways, in case auditioners want to see several different endings.

This is easy to achieve. If you read the first tag line "down," read the next one "up." Two more variations can swiftly be achieved by reading the first "down tag" with a different rhythmic pattern. Then read the "up tag" in another rhythm. In this way you can quickly produce four different tag lines without even thinking much about how to do it.

Do your own thing

Many of the auditions you go to will present you with a part to read that really isn't suitable for you. Agents make mistakes, people get the casting all wrong.

When you see that the part is not really for you, do your own thing. Many students have told us that they never began to succeed until they stopped trying to read like other actors, or like announcers, and just began to "do their own thing." If they spoke like a crow, they did every audition that way. Soon, their crow-like sound began to catch on!

Believing that what you do is good—funny, interesting, right for the part—gives the auditioners confidence. For the most part, agency people do not know exactly what they want. They want you to show them, and they want you to act as though you believe that what you are doing is right. You, the actor, are in charge. You are trying to bring the best out of the words they have written; trying to make their material sound even better than it is.

So be confident. Do your own thing. You can't (as Jean Paul Sartre implied) take someone else's bath!

Vocal Dynamics

Do you talk too loudly? Too softly? Or is your vocal volume just right? That's *dynamics*. And it's a very important element of your delivery when you are auditioning. If you talk too softly you will appear to be very insecure and your energy level will be way down. If you talk too loudly you will appear to be overbearing and your delivery will almost always lack subtlety.

Let's discuss the first problem—too soft. If you do not speak with sufficient volume, some of what you say may be lost to the listener. In addition, the listener will feel that you have little confidence in your product, because speaking softly means to most people that you are unsure of yourself—*and* of what you're selling. Also, it is generally true that "soft speakers" tend to be stone-faced; their faces do not mirror what they are saying. One reason for too-soft speaking is a reluctance to get involved in the copy. It is interesting to watch what generally happens to a soft speaker who is asked to increase his or her volume. As the voice become louder, things begin to happen in the face. It seems that as we increase the energy level needed to give sufficient volume, that same energy brings forth facial expressions that give life to the reading. Now add *really* thinking about what you're saying, and involvement in the copy, plus a winning personality, and you're bound to make an impression.

Sometimes beginning performers ask, "Why should I talk louder? Why not ask the engineer to increase the volume?" There are two reasons. First, when the volume is increased, you are aware as you listen that there has been an electronic increase. There is a different sound to the voice. It does not sound as if the actor had himself increased the volume. Try it yourself on your TV set when you're home watching a commercial and you'll see what we mean. Play it low in volume first, then turn it up. Does it sound as if the actors had suddenly talked louder? We think it will not.

The difficulty with trying to correct the "low volume" or "softness" in your speech lies in the fact that we are often unaware that we are not talking loudly enough. Because we are accustomed to hearing ourselves with little volume, our speech sounds perfectly normal to us. When we are asked to bring our speech up to a normal level it seems to us as if we're shouting.

There are two ways to correct soft speech. The first is to record a commercial on your cassette recorder, using your normal volume. Play it back first at the level you recorded it. Then play it back after turning up the volume. You will hear that it does not really sound as if you had increased the volume as you were speaking.

Now record the commercial with twice the volume you used the first time—maybe even more. Then play them back in sequence. You'll see how your commercial suddenly seems to come to life!

Another method—one that does not require a recorder—is this: Stand in one corner of the room and have someone stand in the opposite corner. Turn on the television set or the radio to your normal listening level. Now read your copy to the person across the room. If you are speaking too softly, they won't be able to hear you. Increase your volume until they *can* hear you, and you'll be producing the volume that should be your normal volume when auditioning.

Talking too loudly is often a problem with a stage actor. Trained to project to the last row in the balcony, the stage actor often does not stop to realize that in radio or TV there is a mike to help out him or her. And like the person who is speaking too softly, the stage actor is not aware of speaking too loudly. For that actor, it is normal delivery.

The way to correct for speech that is too loud is just the opposite of the correction for soft speech. The room you use should be perfectly quiet, with no extraneous noises, just as it would be in a studio. The person delivering the lines should have someone stand facing him or her about three feet away. Now if lines are read at a stage level, the person listening will feel shouted at, and almost instinctively the speaker will adjust the level to a conversational tone. (Remember, do not drop the *energy* level.)

An interesting thing usually happens. Where formerly the speaker was trying to make points with volume, at reduced volume, the speaker finds it necessary to use a wider range of inflections. Consequently, he or she will sound more persuasive. (When you are trying to persuade someone, listen to the broad rise and fall of your voice.) Now the actor who had used a stage delivery must just remember the corrected volume when auditioning.

The procedures we have discussed can be employed to correct the *habitual* soft or loud speaker. There will be commercials where you will be directed to use a great deal of voice—for example, hard-sell commercials for products such as automobiles. And there will be others where you will use reduced volume, such as for wines or perfumes.

Changing Vocal Pitch in a Series

When you are reading a series of words or ideas, you must change your pitch with each word or idea in order to create variety and avoid sounding repetitious. Where you place the words or ideas in your vocal register—low, middle, or high—is up to you.

Take, for example, the series red, white, and blue. A normal reading would be: "Red [low], white [middle], and blue [high]." Or it could be read: "Red [middle], white [low], and blue [high]."

A series of four words might be read: "Apples [low], peaches [middle], pears [low], and bananas [high]," or "Apples [middle], peaches [low], pears [middle], and bananas [high]." It really does not matter as long as there is a change of pitch. So it goes, no matter how many words are in the series.

A word to be emphasized in the middle of a series should be placed highest in your vocal register. For example: "The colors of our country's flag are red [low], white [middle], and blue [high], while the colors of Transylvania's flag are red [low], yellow [high], and blue [middle]."

The same technique applies to a series of ideas. For example: "[low] A firm twin-size mattress, box spring, and bonus frame are only a hundred and ten dollars. [middle] A full-size set is only a hundred and ninety dollars, and [high] a queen-size set is just two hundred and sixty-five dollars." Note that within the first idea there is a word series as well: mattress, box spring, and bonus frame. These must also have a variety of pitch.

Practice changing your pitch with the following:

"It flows on smoothly, evenly, precisely."

"And you'll see your hands look softer, smoother, lovelier. Overnight."

"Fresh, natural, real. Today's kind of sexy."

"There are six kinds: apple, cherry, blueberry, peach, lemon, and pineapple. Get some of each."

Here is a series of ideas:

" 'Z' is for feeling clean as a whistle.

'Z' is for feeling zippy.

'Z' is for feeling terrific.

'Z' is for feeling really clean.

'Z' is for Zooooooom!"

The Free-Flow Method

Many people fall into the trap of trying to read too articulately. They are so careful when they speak that every word stands *alone* and makes their sentence sound choppy. The free-flow method cures this. When you read, just let the natural thoughts tumble out of your mouth as you would in ordinary conversation.

Other actors insist on *breaking their sentences* in just the wrong place. Be sure your pauses are in the places that maintain the *natural flow of thoughts*. Make the spot hang together; don't chop it apart. To help yourself sound less choppy, let one word blend into the next.

Example: "Ifyou'reoneofthosepeoplewhowakeuptiredeverymorning" (pause) "here'sgoodnews."

In using the free-flow method, you must remember that your reading will also be made to sound choppy if your pauses are *too long*. A pause between thoughts should seldom exceed one-quarter second, unless you are doing something in the pause (a gesture, facial expression, or making a nonverbal noise).

When you get rid of overlengthy pauses (usually caused by not learning to look ahead fast enough or losing your place) and let the words flow out in natural conversational rhythms, you will begin to sound as though you were speaking.

Remember, each thought must not be spoken in the same rhythm as the one preceding it. If you do this, you become a victim of the "Ya-ta-ta Ta-ta-ta" Syndrome, and people will know you are reading, not speaking. You can break out of this in two ways: (1) by exaggerating the tonal differences in each sentence (this way, they will not all sound alike); (2) by changing the rhythm of each thought so that you achieve variety.

Eye Contact

Nothing is more important in your delivery to the lens or to a person than "eye contact." If you are reading a commercial for an agent or casting director it is easier for you to concentrate on making eye contact, but the lens is impersonal. It is like the eye of a Cyclops staring at you, and many beginners at the outset are as afraid of the camera as they would be of an actual giant.

When the performer has learned to personalize the lens, that fear will be conquered. Remember, the lens is the person at home viewing your commercial, so if you are auditioning or actually performing the commercial, imagine that you can see your audience in the lens. It is not just looking *at* the lens. You must be trying to *look into it*. The camera will readily pick up the difference in the look that is just in the direction of the camera and the look right down the barrel of the lens.

You cannot escape the "honesty" of the lens. If you are insincere, unsure of yourself, groping for lines, staring at the lens with an immobile face, these all will be very obvious to the viewer. Therefore, if you are delivering your lines from memory you must be very sure of what you are saying. If you have had time to memorize your words thoroughly, there will be no problem, but what if you have not had time to memorize them? If you try to remember and then grope for words, your performance will be dismal. What is the answer?

The Speak-Read Method

This method is to be used when you have not had time to memorize the script.

In order to make your reading "flow" it is important not to have a choppy delivery caused by saying words as individual units (being overarticulate); pausing over and over to find your place; trying to look at your auditioner or the camera all the time.

In using the speak-read method you look down at your copy and memorize as much of the first line as you can, then bring your eyes up and deliver the line to the camera. (Do not lower the head, just the eyes.) Next look down at the script and read right away, without introducing a pause. As you read, you are looking ahead to get more of the copy in your mind. When you are sure of the words, raise your eyes and speak until you run out of words. Then repeat the procedure. If you keep doing this you will maintain a constant flow of dialogue and you will not sound "choppy."

A good way to practice the speak-read method is to focus on a single spot on the wall in front of you and raise your eyes every time to that spot. Really look at the spot as if you were looking *into* a lens, not just in the general direction of it.

After much practice you will find that you will be able to get more and more words in your head. You will *speak* more and *read* less from the page.

When you find you are able to make the copy "flow" easily, you are ready for the next step. The speak-read method merely gets you "up off the page" without regard to proper emphasis. To sell effectively you must be looking into the lens or at your auditioner at the copy points.

Eyes up at Copy Points

What are copy points? The name of the product, what the product does for you, how it feels, how it smells, etc. "When I use *Reveal* it makes my skin feel *soft and smooth*." (The italicized words are the copy points.) You will discover that most of the time the copy points are the punch words. Mark your script with a half-bracket close for each copy point. Now put a half-bracket close at the end of every sentence and at each false period. (Often these will coincide with the copy points.) Practice looking up at these places as you are seated in the reception room going over your copy until you have them fairly well established in your mind.

Now start at the beginning of your copy. Give your slate, holding your gaze into the lens for a brief second at the end of it. Next, look

down at your copy (on the page or cue card) and memorize what you
can. Now look up and deliver your words until you reach your first
copy point. When you have made the point, hold on the lens for a
fraction of a second. This is the difficult part. Until you train yourself
you will very likely look down at the script or card just as you are
finishing the copy point or the last word in the sentence. It is a habit
that derives from our early schooling, when many of us reading out
loud in class were taught to look down as we came to the end of a
sentence so we could look up and into the faces of the students as we
started the next line. The correct procedure is to hold on the lens for
a moment at the copy point or end of the sentence and then look
down and resume reading as quickly as you can, as you did in the
speak-read method. Do not take the time to raise your eyes from the
text. It may seem to you that the pause thus created is too long. But
remember, you cannot see your eyes. If they are making contact and
saying something, the only actual "dead spot" (or pause) is the time
it takes to return to the copy and get started again.

To perfect this technique, practice looking in a mirror. If you find
you are looking at yourself at a copy point or end of a line, obviously
your eyes must be up from the text. It's as simple as that. As you
continue to practice you will discover that you can get up from the
text faster and retain more and more words, and the copy points will
become so obvious they will fairly "jump out at you" from the text.

You must also remember to have your eyes up and hold on the lens
every time you are asking a question. If your eyes are down on the
copy it will appear that they are closed. Would you ask a question of
someone and close your eyes at the end of the question? Of course
not. Nor should you do so when asking a question of the viewer.

When you have practiced the speak-read method and become
really adept at keeping your eyes up at the copy points, your delivery
will be almost as effective as complete memorization.

Accompanying Thoughts with Facial Expressions

After you have determined the copy points in the script and are able
to hold your eyes on the camera when you deliver them, there is one
more very important step in developing an effective delivery. A

change of facial expression must accompany each change of thought. If your face does not mirror your change of thought, you will not achieve the variety necessary to be effective. You will be giving a "poker face" delivery. To illustrate this, try the following:

First make a *question* face. "Do you suffer from sleepless nights?" (Then do a *good news* face.) "Then here's good news." (Now an *explanation* face.) "Now medical science has perfected Someesa." (Now go to a *remarkable* face.) "A remarkable aid to sleep . . . " (Now a *gentle* face.) "Someesa gently pulls the shades down on daytime cares". Note that there were (or should be) five different faces in the first few lines. Remember, however, that excessive use of facial expressions in a close-up may look grotesque. The longer the shot (the farther you seem to be from the camera), the broader the facial expressions can be.

In addition, remember this: People usually tell you with their faces what they are going to say *before* they say it. For example, the doctor with bad news—you know he has bad news. The woman getting ready to impart a secret—you know she's going to get confidential. Performers look more realistic when their facial expressions precede by miniseconds the thought they are about to speak. Try it. It works.

Wearing Glasses at Auditions

Glasses can be used as a prop. Start without them. Put them on after the introduction. Take them off before you deliver the last line. If you do it smoothly, it is a very theatrical device.

To kill *reflections,* you can push the back of the frames up from your eyes toward the crown of your head.

If you can't see the cue card, ask to have it moved in, or ask, "May I work from the script?"

Use glasses with nonreflecting frames. For men, auditioners seem to prefer black frames or rims.

One-Line and No-Line Commercials and Pantomime

If you were to make a survey, you'd probably discover that about 50 to 60 percent of all commercials involve no lines of dialogue, or just one line for each of the actors on camera. These commercials are cast primarily by type, and you're either the right type or you aren't. When you walk through the door of the audition room, the advertising agency people and the client immediately say to themselves "yes," or "no." So no matter how well you read whatever lines there are, you don't have a chance if they don't think you are the type.

Of the twenty people seen for each one-line or no-line spot, probably ten were not really the type and shouldn't have been sent at all. Of the remaining ten, five will be judged as not the type they had in mind by the client, the copywriter, or the art director. Those left may get a "call-back" to read again, and it is at this point that acting ability comes into play. Even though you may have no lines at all, acting is still important.

After all, you don't just stand there and smile when you're doing a commercial with no lines. You are always asked to do something. Sneeze. Rub your eyes. Put drops in them. Eat an imaginary bowl of cereal and enjoy it. The list of things you could be asked to do is endless.

A large number of pantomimes deal with various kinds of illness: colds, headache, fever. Watch the commercials on television for common medicines, and practice the faces and gestures you see.

Another large group involves eating—tasting. How do you hold a cup? How do you put a spoon in your mouth? Notice how you do these things, and practice re-creating them without the "props."

Should you use pantomime at an audition? Don't if it gets in the way of a good reading. If you do, avoid meaningless gestures. Some actors will hold up an imaginary package of detergent and keep it there throughout the entire audition. They look like the Statue of Liberty without her torch—the gesture is meaningless. A good rule is to use pantomime if the script is telling about physical things you are doing. For example: "Just twist off the top, apply the lotion to your hand. Makes your skin feel smooth! Now smell it. What fragrance!" If you are *saying* all this without *doing* anything, the viewer feels that something is missing. How much more effective if you pretend to remove an imaginary top, pretend you put a drop on your hand. Now rub the skin that has been lotioned with the other hand, then raise your hand to your nose and take a whiff, and of course break into a pleasant smile. If you are using effective, illustrative pantomime and others at the audition are just reciting their lines with their bare faces hanging out, your pantomime could be the deciding factor in your winning the audition. (Of course, be sure that everything you do is seen by the lens. Know your frame.)

So employ pantomime if the script cries out for it and if the pantomime will add to the reality of the situation, but don't just wave your arms around in meaningless gestures. That is worse than doing nothing.

When asked to pantomime driving a car, for example, some actors pretend to grasp the wheel, then make exaggerated turning movements, first right and then left. Try that on the road someday and see what happens. You'll be in a ditch in fifteen seconds! Pantomime must look real! The only way to learn it is to become observant about your daily conduct. How do you hold an automobile wheel? How do you talk to a person seated next to you in the front seat of the car? Do you turn to him full face or do you look at him out of the corner of your eye occasionally?

Often pantomime precedes the one line of copy. For example, you sniffle and say, "My nose is all stuffed up." Or you scratch and say, "This darned itching . . . how can I get relief? Or, perhaps, you are seen watering the lawn, then you turn toward the camera and say, "Boy! This grass never looked better, thanks to Regal Fertilizer!"

An actress once earned twenty-seven thousand dollars with only one line. All she had to say at the audition was, "Now I can breathe again." But before she said it, she did the following:

- Looked at the camera as if she had a bad cold. This involved a heavy, tired eye, open mouth (she could not breathe through her nose, could she?), a sneeze here and there, a headache.
- Reached for this new nasal decongestant.
- Looked at it to see what it said it could do.
- Uncapped it.

- Used it in each nostril.
- Looked at the camera again as if the decongestant didn't help.
- Took a few sniffs to see if her nasal passages were opening.
- Was pleased (slowly) to discover that they were.
- Took a big breath (raised her shoulders so the audience could see that she did breathe).
- As she exhaled, she said the line with a sign of relief: "Now I can breathe again."

But the only instruction the actress actually got was: "Look at the camera as if you had a cold. Reach for the decongestant. Try it. Get relief and say the line." (All the rest was her own invention, and it won the audition for her.)

How many "scenes" were there in that one line? Ten. But most actors would have compressed it into two or three actions (or scenes). Good actors take their time. They carve out their plan of action cleanly, and they show the audience in a believable way exactly what is happening. In that way they win one-line commercials.

As a practice exercise, ask a friend to hand you an imaginary cookie. The chances are that his thumb and index finger will be touching each other. This shows that the cookie had a zero thickness! Take the cookie from him. Then begin to chew it and ask yourself how long you really would have to chew and taste *before* you could say, "Hey, this is really a great cookie!"

A few years ago, a commercial for a famous brand of peanut butter required an actress to take a taste of the peanut butter from a spoon and immediately say, "Tastes more like real peanut butter." It was so obvious that she hadn't had time to taste it that the company got letters to that effect from viewers. It may not, however, have been the fault of the actress. The director may have said, "We're tight on time, so as soon as you put the spoon in your mouth, say the line. Nobody will notice that you haven't taken time to taste it." Nobody noticed but the viewers!

How do you learn good pantomime? If you consider that all commercial pantomime is based upon five simple principles, you will be well on your way to understanding how to do it well. To make your pantomime look real, you must take into consideration:

- The *weight* of the object: If you hold a suitcase, your arm and body should reflect the weight.

- The *shape* of the object: Holding up a package of something? How big should it look in your hands?
- Time: If you taste something, how long does it really take to determine if you like it or you don't? If you're looking at something, how long does it take to register on your face before you comment on the scene?
- Friction: How do you pull open a door? Open a drawer? Push a baby carriage? Use an iron to smooth a shirt?
- Common sense: Ask yourself where you are and what you are doing. How do you *really* do it?

If you consider these five factors when doing any pantomime, you should do it well, especially if you practice at home.

Following is a list of suggested pantomimes for you to practice.

Practice Pantomimes

- Food: Eating soup from a spoon. Drinking hot coffee. Eating spaghetti. Drinking a cool drink from a glass, or from a bottle. Licking an ice-cream cone.
- Food preparation: Icing a cake. Opening a can, or a bottle, or a pop top. Pouring liquid. Measuring ingredients.
- Illness: Coughing. Massaging temples. Moving with a backache. Showing symptoms of nasal congestion. Sneezing.
- Grooming: Shaving. Combing hair. Washing hair. Gargling. Spraying mouthwash.
- Aromas: Bacon frying. Cat box needs cleaning. Burning food. Perfume. Freshly washed clothes.

There are innumerable actions and expressions that will help you to give a favorable pantomimed audition. Get your cues from commercials you see. Think up some situations of your own, and practice in front of a mirror.

Answers to
Four Keys
Exercises

Punch Answers

Always thought noodles were all the <u>same</u>? Well, the <u>next</u> time you're in the <u>market</u>, take a peek in the window of a package of <u>Ratazzi Egg Noodles</u>. <u>Here's</u> what you'll <u>see</u>. <u>Golden noodles</u>! <u>Rich</u>, <u>golden noodles</u>—the color of the <u>yolks</u> of <u>country-fresh eggs</u>. And that's exactly where <u>Ratazzi Egg Noodles</u> get their <u>color</u>. They're made with <u>golden yolks</u>. Only <u>egg yolks</u>! And when you lift <u>Ratazzi Egg Noodles</u> out of the <u>cooking pot</u>, <u>pile</u> 'em on a <u>platter</u>, <u>drizzle</u> 'em with <u>butter</u>—you'll find they're the <u>tenderest</u> noodles, the <u>lightest</u>, <u>tastiest</u> noodles you've <u>ever</u> eaten. <u>Ratazzi Egg Noodles</u>. Pay just a <u>little more</u> and you get the <u>best</u>.

Years ago kids were <u>nibblers</u>—and they're <u>still</u> nibblers. <u>Kids</u> haven't <u>changed</u>. But what's <u>in</u> some of the things they're <u>nibbling</u>? <u>That's</u> changed. For the <u>worse</u>. Harmful <u>stabilizers</u> or <u>preservatives</u> have been <u>added</u>. But <u>not</u> to <u>Snappy Jack</u>. It's all <u>natural</u> ingredients. <u>Wholesome</u> <u>carmel-coated popcorn</u>—<u>nutritious peanuts</u>. <u>100</u> percent natural. <u>Nothing</u> <u>artificial</u>. So <u>let</u> 'em nibble. As long as it's <u>Snappy Jack</u>.

Color Marking Answers

Sooner or later you'll try one of our White Eagle cigars, and when you do, we're gonna (getcha)! Maybe with our (mild) (aroma)—maybe with our (sweet) (taste). But we're gonna (getcha). Real (good).

Bott puts the taste of (luscious) (sun-drenched) Florida oranges in new Bott Orange Soda. (Mouth-watering) Concord (grapes) in new (Grape Soda). (Ripe,) (juicy,) (raspberries) in new Bott (Raspberry Soda).

Inflection Exercise No. 1—Answers

Grand National Bank works. With this country's leading companies. All along the food-production chain. To help provide food. For consumers. In every state. In the union. Countries all around the world.

After "works" we have a complete thought—a subject and a verb. Now note the phrases that amplify the original thought. They begin with (in order) a preposition, an adverb, an infinitive, a preposition, a preposition, and a preposition. Remember, look for the prepositions, adverbs, infinitives, and conjunctions in your copy. Make a vocal period—a false period—in front of them. As we have said, you need not always pause for a false period; in fact, in most cases you do not pause. Your voice merely slides down to denote the period and you continue on without a pause. In the above copy the only pause, and just a brief one, should occur after "chain."

Inflection Exercise No. 2—Answers

These are the hands that wash the baby. The hands that soak the diapers, scrub the crib, wash the dress. Baby looks beautiful. But look at those hands. Red. Rough. Harsh to the touch. Hands like these need medicated Lotiana. The hardworking cream. For hands that work hard. Lotiana not only softens and smooths, but actually helps heal. As no ordinary lotion can. Works so fast. You can almost feel it start to heal. And you'll see your hands look softer, smoother, lovelier. Overnight. Remember, a woman's hands have to be soft and smooth. For so many reasons. Keep yours looking their loveliest. With Lotiana skin cream. The hardworking cream. For hands that work hard.

The opening line suggests that the copywriter may be paralleling "This is the house that Jack built." So a false period is called for. If the copywriter is at the audition (many times one is present), then she or he will be impressed with the fact that you got the parallel. Now, on "diapers" and "crib," use exaggerated sliding-upward inflections to indicate the monotony and drudgery of the tasks. "Red. Rough. Harsh to the touch" become three separate billboards. ". . . not only softens and smooths" indicates that the thought is not complete without the next clause, so there is a sliding-upward inflection on "smooths." Use sliding-upward inflections on "softer, smoother." The billboard is too "punchy" for those words.

Transition Exercise—Answers: No. 1

I'm a terrible cook, really I am. But do you know, my pies always turn out wonderful! What I'm proudest of is the crust. It's so light and flaky. But I can't take credit for it, because it's Crispit that does it. Every time! Boy, I can remember when the water problem had me stumped—how much to put in? But now with Crispit there's no guesswork, and my pies are always light and flaky. Believe me, I know from experience, Crispit makes pie crust crisp.

No. 2

For countertops, choose Topcote. ⌐Topcote laminated plastic gives you original designs and beautiful permanent colors. ⌐It is heat-resistant, safe from acid and water, and greaseproof.

⌐Look at this dream kitchen. ⌐Topcote is so easy to keep clean and shiny—just like new, ⌐and Topcote is so decorative. ⌐This vanity will always be safe from cosmetic stains. ⌐This kitchen will be the envy of your neighbors. ⌐Throughout your house use Topcote for all your countertops.

Practicing with Cue Cards at Home

How can you practice with cue cards at home? Obviously, you can't print a dozen or so cards. It's time-consuming and costly. But when you stop to think about it, any script in the book, held at a distance of 1½ feet from your eyes, is the same size (to your eyes) as a large cue card 8 feet from your eyes. So prop up one of the scripts from the book, pretend it is a cue card, and practice speak-read to your heart's content.

Some Final
Pointers

Memorization for Recordings

Before you begin to memorize, thoroughly analyze your commercial, then prepare your reading exactly the way you intend to deliver it.

Next, read the commercial many times, trying to look up from the copy as much as possible. You will find that words and phrases will begin to stick in your memory. For portions that seem difficult, examine the meaning closely and paraphrase, then return to the actual copy.

As you begin to look up from the copy, fix your eyes on a single point of reference, which will become the lens when you are delivering your commercial. This will concentrate and minimize your peripheral vision, so that when you come to the studio your "memory bank" is not filled with images of your home surroundings. You may say, "I knew it at home," and you did; but new surroundings can cause distractions you may not be aware of.

Have someone at home cue you on your lines, prompting you where you seem really stuck for the word or line.

Take more than one day to prepare the memorization. Lines quickly learned tend to fade quickly. On the second day of preparation, try to recite your commercial early in the morning, while you're still sleepy. Read the lines to yourself on a bus or a subway, with all the distractions that will be present.

Always ask for a rehearsal at an audition. You will generally be given one. Rehearse only to the lens, shutting out as many distractions as possible.

Remember, concentration is the most important key to the memorization and retention of lines.

One excellent way to memorize is to record the commercial and play it back over and over. Isn't this the way kids learn words to rock songs?

The TelePrompTer

The TelePrompTer is a machine that moves a scroll from bottom to top on a device that is usually positioned just above or below the camera lens. The scroll contains the entire commercial and sometimes stage directions for the performers. A movable indicator (red arrow or other) is located on the left side of the TelePrompTer. It points to the line the actor is delivering at the moment and is positioned nearest to the lens. Thus the indicator would be high when the TelePrompTer is below the lens, and low when above, so that the eyes appear to be looking into the lens.

An operator keeps the scroll moving at the pace established by the performer, so that the current line is opposite the indicator. A good operator will always have the line at the right place and will not exceed your pace. If you feel you are being rushed, it is because the lines are always moving upward. Maintain your pace—don't feel you must hurry.

Look at the TelePrompTer just as you would look at the lens—that is, just as if you were looking at a person. Do not stare or narrow your eyes. If you cannot read the letters, which are 1-inch high, you are in trouble. Then you must memorize or wear contacts, or ask for "idiot cards," which have large lettering.

When you have to look away from the TelePrompTer and then back again, it is helpful to have a mark placed on the TelePrompTer script, such as a bracket close for leaving the TelePrompTer and a bracket open for coming back. Carry a red magic marker with you. The operator must make the appropriate marks. It's a regulation of his union.

If you wish to deliver part of the text from memory, looking directly into the lens, and only using the TelePrompTer for a difficult or involved passage, make sure that you look away, perhaps at the product, before making the shift, so that the change of eye angle will be less noticeable.

Some actors prefer to keep their eyes on the TelePrompTer even though they have thoroughly memorized the commercial. Then there is no shift of eyes, and the fact that they have memorized the copy keeps their delivery from sounding as though they were reading.

Today some TelePrompTers "crawl the words" right over the lens. You can see them, but the audience can't, so when you look at the text, you are actually looking directly into the lens.

Don't try to "go on memory" while looking at the TelePrompTer script. Read it. Otherwise, it may throw you. If you are reading the

TelePrompTer through the entire script, find a place or two where you can look away. This will help prevent a "TelePrompTer stare" and help the illusion that you are not reading from a script.

You will, of course, have rehearsals before filming or taping a commercial, but practice with the TelePrompTer operator before camera rehearsal. When you are through with dressing and makeup, look for the TelePrompTer operator and ask him or her to rehearse with you. You are not imposing. The operator is being paid to serve you.

Remember, the copy (usually in all capital letters) will look different from the typed script. Run through the TelePrompTer script with the operator several times. Then you'll be all set for the camera rehearsal.

You will never have a TelePrompTer at an audition. You see, the TelePrompTer is leased, and along with the TelePrompTer on a day of shooting goes its operator, whose services are charged to the production company. This would all be too costly for an audition operation.

How often will you have a TelePrompTer at a shooting? It's hard to say. Maybe 50 percent of the time if you are a spokesperson and have a lot of copy. It always is a good idea after you have received your script to check with the ad agency or production company to ascertain if there will be a TelePrompTer on the set. (Obviously don't call to check if you have only one line!)

Some performers hate the TelePrompTer; others love it. Those who hate it feel that they get a more one-to-one communication by looking directly into the lens. They feel that when they read they are not as natural as when the lines are delivered from memory. But remember, nobody *makes* you use the TelePrompTer. It is your choice. But even if you are delivering lines from memory, the TelePrompTer is useful during rehearsals. If you forget your line, check the TelePrompTer. This does not upset the flow or timing of the segment you are rehearsing. (Of course, the shift of eyes from lens to TelePrompTer would not be acceptable in an actual take.)

To some performers the TelePrompTer is a godsend. No more worries about forgetting lines. Actors become so proficient using the TelePrompTer that they are more relaxed and natural than when looking at the lens.

You might ask, "Why should I memorize my script if I know I can use the TelePrompTer?" Well, memorization is more than just learning the words—it is also working out how you are going to say them. The performer who has not memorized the script before using the TelePrompter almost always sounds "read-y." So Tele-PrompTer or no TelePrompTer, memorize your copy.

How to Handle . . .

Nerves

"I'd love to do commercials, and everybody says I'm a great commercial type, but I get so nervous in front of people, I'd just go all to pieces!"

Yes, "nerves" can be a problem—that is, the *displaying* of nerves. But nerves are the stuff a good performance is made of. Nerves are the driving force that produce the energy you need when auditioning or shooting a commercial. Without them you'll come over as a clod, and there's little call for wooden Indians these days.

So you have "nerves." Be thankful for them, but learn how to control them. First, you can't "take something" for them. You can't swallow an "upper" or a "downer" and expect to give a good audition. There are, however, certain physical things you can do to prepare for that time when you want to appear calm and cool.

Have you ever noticed that one of the first indications of nervousness is shortness of breath? Since the diaphragm controls breathing, it's probably the most important muscle in the body to an actor. Hence a performer must learn to breathe from the diaphragm and do regular exercises to strengthen it. When we take a shallow breath, just filling the tops of our lungs, we soon run out of breath, especially when we're nervous. When we breathe from the diaphragm, the diaphragm pushes down, enlarging the lung cavity, and the lungs draw in much more air. We have taken a "deep" breath and should now have sufficient air supply.

Now for the exercises. The first is a simple deep-breathing exercise. Lie flat on your back on the floor. Relax as if you were preparing to sleep. Although we may not realize it, we breathe correctly, from the diaphragm, as we sleep. Notice that as you relax, the center of your torso is pushing upward. As the diaphragm pushes *downward* it also pushes *outward*. Slowly take a dozen deep breaths, holding each breath for a count of five before releasing the air, and then slowly release the air—don't let it rush out. Now practice that same exercise standing, making sure the diaphragm is pushing out.

The next exercise is also simple. Lie on the floor with your knees bent and do sit-ups. Daily increase the number of sit-ups until you can do at least fifty without stopping. This exercise strengthens both the stomach muscles and the diaphragm.

"My, all this physical training just to do a commercial?" Yes, you will need all the breath reserve you can muster, especially at first, when you are likely to be the most nervous. And what if you are doing a film narration where you may be speaking almost nonstop for a couple of hours? It takes more strength and energy than you can imagine until you've done it. Have you ever noticed that when people are ill they hardly have the energy to speak? Breathing properly takes strength, so work on it.

Now you're at the audition. You're facing the camera. It's staring at you. And your auditioner is staring at you. They're both just waiting for you to make your first mistake. Right? Wrong. As we've mentioned earlier, it is in the best interests of the auditioner to get the best performance possible from you. It makes the auditioner look good in the eyes of the agency and the sponsor. We also suggested that you think of the camera as a person. You have a message for that person—a message that might mean a great improvement in that person's life-style. The only thing that matters for the next thirty seconds is that you deliver that message clearly and forcefully. To do that you must be involved in what you are saying, and when you are really involved and concentrating on conveying your message, there is little time to worry about how you look. Are your hair and makeup all right? Is your tie straight? Nor can you be thinking of how your auditioner is appraising you. When you are involved you will also involve the person you are talking to, the one at home who is watching your commercial (or will be one day, you hope).

"Gee, I was doing fine until I held up the product, and then my hand began to shake!" Yes, that may happen. It's when we have to hold our hand still in one position that nerves seem to take over and produce shaking. Try to work out your business so you never have to hold your hand still for very long. When the hand is moving it is not only less likely to shake, but if there is any shaking it won't be noticed because of the motion. If you are pouring a cup of coffee, for instance, instead of holding the cup still, try slowly lifting the cup as you pour. It will reduce any shaking to the minimum and at least the tremor will not be noticed.

If ever you are on the set shooting a commercial and the director asks you to hold a product in a fixed position for a considerable length of time while the shot is lighted, politely try to get out of doing it by suggesting that someone else stand in for you. Say, "I'm afraid if I hold the product for you my hand may shake when we're doing the take." We know of a case where this actually happened. The director asked a girl to hold the product during lighting. She demurred, telling the director she was afraid of what might happen during the take if she complied. The director said, "Oh, don't be such a prima donna. After all, what are we paying you for?" She had to hold her hand still for about five minutes. Sure enough, when it came to the take, her hand was shaking so badly a hand model had to be called in to get the shot. It served the director right!

Meanwhile, back at the audition, you've slated, started the copy, and on the second line you stumble and misread. What to do? First, what *not* to do. Don't take the time to chastise yourself mentally. At this point we all feel like saying to ourselves, "You dummy! What did you do that for?" And we may even make the grimace that goes with the thought, and that will surely display our nervousness and insecurity. If the bobble occurs early in the script, just stop and say, "May I start over?" What are they going to say? "No"? When they say, as they surely will, "Sure, start from the top," then ask, "Shall I reslate?" (All of this procedure stalls for time and helps you collect your nerves.) So you do or don't reslate and you start again, first checking the spot where you stumbled on your script or cue card. If your bobble occurs *late* in the copy, don't stop. If it's just a little slip, don't even bother about it, just go on. If it's important, go back and correct it without batting an eyelid. Your face must never show that you are the least bit ill at ease. The important thing to remember in an audition is that you are being judged on your style, personality, and delivery. You're not expected to be letter-perfect at an audition. (Of course, don't stumble all over the place, either!) And remember, if you don't show your nerves, how are they going to know you're nervous?

Well, you got through the audition, and glory be! You won. Now for the shoot. Play it like the audition. The camera is your only audience. "But what about all those guys standing there watching me, the crew? They look like they're just waiting for me to make a mistake." They're not. Let's look at it positively. They're waiting and hoping for you to do it right. You might think that they'd like you to blow lines so the shoot can extend into overtime. Not so. They want to get home for dinner.

"Passes"

You may ask, "If I go out into the big, bad world of show business, is someone going to make a pass at me?" Very likely. (But try not to be too disappointed if they don't.) The following advice about unwanted (or wanted) advances may be very elementary, but it is good to keep in mind.

Dear Agatha: I have heard that the road to success in film work and commercials is via the "casting couch." Is it true?
Signed,
Cynical

Dear Cynical: Not true. Some years ago actresses at times became film stars not because of their acting ability but because of their relationship with the producer. In feature films today, an actress must give a good performance on the screen—not in the bedroom. The "casting couch" may be the road to an initial and inconsequential success that may well jeopardize future important achievements. Maybe you will be given a very small role to play or a job as an extra. In the minds of the production company, you will be thought of as "the girlfriend," or worse yet, "*a* girlfriend" of the producer, not capable of assuming more important roles. So don't stare at stardom from a reclining position. Be sure you are on your feet when you're gazing at stars.
Sincerely,
Agatha

Dear Agatha: I am single but the account executive who interviewed me in the advertising agency is a married man, and he—

Stop right there! We can finish the story. And he said, "I am married, but we're getting a divorce." This is the road to heartbreak. Wait until he plumps the divorce papers in your hands. After that let your conscience be your guide.

Dear Agatha: I read for a commercial yesterday and the casting director wants me to come in next week and read for the producer. He also wants to take me to lunch. Should I go? I am thirty-one, married with two children.
Signed,
Doubtful

Dear Doubtful: If you live in a city where everything that goes on is everybody's business, beware. The luncheon date may be the most innocent meeting in the world, but if being seen with someone other than your husband means it will spread all over town, avoid it. On the other hand, if your luncheon is not going to hit the front pages of your local *Morning Journal*, a luncheon can become the means of getting to know influential people better. To forestall a pass, be sure to take along the pictures of your children and brandish them about the time the coffee arrives. Nothing can so put a damper on "romance openers" as bragging about "the little ones."
Sincerely,
Agatha

Since you obviously do not want to offend important people you are turning down, always be sure your way of saying "no" is a pleasant one. Usually all you have to say is, "Having dinner with you does sound very pleasant, but I'm involved (married) (engaged)."

Don't be a wiseacre and try to be cute about your turndown. We know of an actress who used to say, "I'd love to go out with you but you see I'm doing secret work for the President, and if he knew I'd swung with you, he'd never trust me again." No one likes a smart aleck, as this actress soon discovered when the calls stopped coming in.

Be gracious in your rebuffs, but firm. Don't fall for, "Come over to my apartment tonight. I've got a new record I want you to hear." Carve out your career in your waking hours, not your sleeping hours. Remember, you lose respect when you grant sexual favors to gain employment. Make it a point to be hired for your ability, not your *avail*ability.

Unions

You may have seen the commercial that played all over the country at one time where the people interviewed had trouble spelling the world "relief." They all spelled it "R-o-l-a-i-d-s." Some people have difficulty when it comes to spelling the word "union." Some spell it "u-n-f-a-i-r" (those who have difficulty getting in). Others spell it "u-n-s-t-i-n-t-i-n-g" (these are the union members who know that their union bends every effort to negotiate the best wages and working conditions that can be attained for them).

There are five show-biz unions: Actors Equity Association, the American Guild of Musical Artists, the American Guild of Variety Artists, the Screen Actors Guild, and the American Federation of Television and Radio Artists. The last two, SAG (or "the Guild") and AFTRA, as they are known in the trade, are the two unions with jurisdiction in the field of commercials, film, and live and taped TV and radio. These are the two unions you will have to deal with in the work you are seeking.

How Do I Get into a Union?

Perhaps in your area there is no union, so you have no problem. There is even nonunion production in commercials and film in New York and other large metropolitan areas where SAG exists, casting actors from the pool of talent that has not been accepted into the Guild. Producers contact the TV schools in New York, where they have learned that they can find good performers with no union affiliation. You see, many actors come to New York with real professional experience under their belts: local TV shows, dinner theaters, and repertory companies, experience on radio stations, etc. They may have had much more acting training and experience than the "Broadway" actor whose only claim to fame may be an occasional off-Broadway or off-off-Broadway play. So when you first come to New York, seek out nonunion work. It could tide you over until you get into a union and can then get union employment.

But you certainly don't want to stay nonunion. You need the prestige of a union affiliation to help you get work, and you aren't going to make the "big bucks" in nonunion work. What do you do?

First you join AFTRA, by paying an initiation fee and current dues. Then after one year you may automatically join SAG if you have worked under AFTRA's jurisdiction within that period, in a small part in a soap opera, an "under five" (meaning less than five lines), or a part on any radio commercial, for example.

The second means of entry to SAG is by means of a waiver. Here's how it works. You audition for a commercial. You get the audition either through your own efforts or are sent by an agent. The casting director decides that you and only you would be *just marvelous*" for the part. Quotes and italics for this reason: In applying for a waiver for you, the casting director must assure the Guild (SAG) that you and *only* you will do for the part—you have the "just right" look—or better yet, you have a special skill that is needed for the role you are to play. If you are a tightrope walker and that's what they're looking for, you're in.

A waiver can also be applied for if the performer can prove he or she is truly a professional. Having attended an acting school or a TV school helps, but you will generally need more than that. If you are a member of Actors Equity, or have performed extensively in non-union regional theaters, that should be enough to demonstrate your professionalism.

Yes, there's a way to get in, and it works on countless occasions, but how do you get the interview with the agency caster or the agent in the first place? Aye, there's the rub.

As we have mentioned, your picture and résumé are your entry. If your picture comes on like Gang Busters, if your résumé shows that you are a serious performer with experience (and local experience is given a great deal of weight), and if you have that special skill they are looking for, it's a good bet they'll call you in.

But what about the agent? How do I get past the receptionist if she says only union actors are interviewed? Again, your picture and résumé. If they're impressive, they can open the doors for you. It is not that agents have anything against nonunion talent, it is just that they do not have the time to see every Tom, Dick, and Harry who would like to have an agent submit them for commercials.

But if the agent will not see nonunion talent, just old union members, where does new talent come from? In the first place, the interview, perhaps augmented with a "cold" reading of a commercial on the part of a performer, is not nearly as good an indication of what the performer can do as seeing that actor in an actual performance. So now we come to the showcases we mentioned earlier. If an agent thinks an off-Broadway or off-off-Broadway play is worth the time and effort, or if he or she is especially interested in a performer in the play, that agent will likely take the time to attend.

Then there are the commercial showcases run by the various TV schools. The agent will take the time to attend them, knowing that, as in the case of the Weist-Barron Commercial Showcase, the actor has had prior training in commercials at the school and has passed an audition to prove himself or herself qualified to be in the showcase. Then the agent knows it will not be a waste of time—a case of spending a couple of hours hearing a bunch of actors who *think* they can do commercials.

For a moment, let's get back to the actor who spells "union" "u-n-f-a-i-r." All that is necessary is to get an audition, alone or through an agent, win that audition, and then get the waiver. Right? Not so fast. An agency casting director might tell you, "Why, just the other day I was looking for a female contortionist, a surfboarder, a hang-glider pilot, and a one-legged man. I looked through my files, found them all, called them in, auditioned them, applied for waivers, and they were all accepted by the Guild!" What the casting director did not say was, "The other day, I was auditioning for a housewife. It came down to two women, both of whom would have been just right for the part—great looks, great personality, great delivery. One was union, the other nonunion. Since it was really a tie, I chose the union member. Why go through all the work of a waiver? Besides, the client was in a hurry to shoot, and by choosing the union member, everything was all set."

Fair, or unfair? The nonunion performer would opt for the latter, but the union member would say, "It's fair. After all, I've been through the mill. I came in the hard way. I pay my dues. In a close decision, I should be given the edge." (SAG calls it "preference of employment.") And that's what *you'll* say when you become a union member. Right now, you're on the outside looking in.

But there's yet another Catch-22 to this waiver business. It has to do with the agent. The agent wants to send an actor to the audition whom he or she thinks will have a good chance of winning. Let's say five auditionees have been asked for. Should the agent send five union members, or four union members and one nonunion member? Maybe the nonunion member will not be considered because of all that business about a waiver.

There are those in SAG who feel that the present entrance requirements are too stringent and that they promote nonunion production. After all, if all the good commercial performers are in the union, where would the nonunion producers find talent? What if the entrance requirement were that actors must first win an audition and then, with a performance contract in their pocket, join the Guild? Would not winning a commercial be proof of acceptability? "Ah," say the naysayers, "but then wives and sweethearts will be cast instead of competent actors!" A point. After all, a well-known Cadillac dealer in New York *did* use his wife in commercials, and she was OK. But can we believe that many sponsors would jeopardize their commercials with inadequate performers?

At present there is no movement extant in SAG to bring about a change in the entrance system. The main reasons are that there have been no complaints from the ad agencies as to the talent pool, nor have there been many complaints from the agencies about the refusal of SAG to grant waiver requests. So it seems that everyone is satisfied . . . except the actor who "wants in."

Lest all of the above discourage you from coming to New York, we must hasten to say if you are talented—*really* talented—then New York is the place to take advantage of it. At Weist-Barron (and we're sure other schools) we have seen actor after actor go to the top after being trained, and then exposed to agents through the Agents' Commercial Showcase. You might make it even without training, if you have an outstanding personality and have developed a great delivery with the help of this book. But we would not be fair if we tried to tell you that the road to commercial success is called "Easy Street."

TV Commercials Payments

In one year one actor made $75,000 doing a toothpaste commercial, another earned $35,000 doing a sleep aid, another was paid $125,000 on a dishwashing liquid, another $15,000 for a cleanser, and still another was paid $300 for a soap commercial. Why the wide range in remuneration? Well, the first actor's commercial was used in what is called a "nationwide saturation campaign"—it was used all over the country, many, many times. The second actor's commercial was used nationwide but was not played as many times. The third actor had an exclusive contract with the sponsor, which meant that the actor could perform for no one else. The fourth actor was not used on every commercial produced by the sponsor. The fifth actor performed in a commercial which was never used. It was "shelved" by the sponsor, who decided after viewing the finished product that it would not do the job. Another commercial was made in its place, so the actor got paid just for the day's work.

Since there is such a wide variance in what actors can receive (stars can make much more than the above figures), it is most difficult to give you an estimate of the amount of money you can make from commercials. One large New York ad agency estimates that the average commercial nets the performer between $5,000 and $7,500 a year. Performers in demand can do many commercials and thus end up with a substantial amount of money. There is, however, a catch. It is called a "conflict." A Pepsi-Cola actor, for instance, cannot do another "drink" commercial; an Ivory Soap actor cannot perform on a Palmolive commercial. Many times a company that has a wide range of products will not allow an actor to do a commercial for a competing company. At the time of the audition the actor must state whether he or she has a conflict, or the actor can get in serious trouble. Actors have been sued when they have accepted a conflict resulting in two competing commercials on the air at the same time.

In these pages we will try not to become too technical in our explanation of how payments are made, and we will deal only with payments made under SAG or AFTRA. Nonunion payments will vary with your locale and the amount you can negotiate. For a complete rundown you should consult your local union office, if there is one in your area, and of course if you are doing union work.

To begin with, you are paid for your time. The "on camera" actor is paid for a day's work: an eight-hour day, with overtime payments if he or she works longer. The "voice-over" actor is paid for a two-hour period called a "session fee." In each case an additional full payment is made for any other commercial made within that span of time. Also, in each case, the amount you receive for making the commercial constitutes the first "use fee."

And what is the use fee? First let's discuss Class A program use. If a commercial is played nationally within the body of a program, the actor receives a payment for every time it is used. (For program usage see the schedule below.) These reuse fees are called "residuals," and a schedule of their payments is set up by the unions. (*Note:* SAG and AFTRA co-negotiate the commercials contract, so payments are identical.) It is Class A residual use that piles up the money for the actor—the more use, the more money.

A commercial played *between* programs (station-break time) is termed a "wild spot," and the actor involved receives a payment for thirteen weeks of unlimited use of the spot, the payment varying with the area covered by the spot. The reasoning behind the lesser payment for the use of the commercial is that during a change of programs the viewer may not be "glued to the set." It is known in the industry as "B and B" time—that is, Beer and Bathroom time.

A third classification is Dealer Use: usually a six-month buy-out with unlimited use.

Schedule of Payments for TV Commercials*

Principals†

Class A on camera Uses	Class A off camera (voice-over) Uses
1st $300.00 (day's work)	1st $225.60 (session fee)
2nd $115.95	2nd $90.75
3rd through 13th $92.00	3rd through 13th $72.15
14 and over @ $44.10	14 and over @ $32.75

*In effect through 1984 with possible cost-of-living increases.

†A principal is generally the one delivering the message, but it can be anyone who fits all three of these qualifications: identifiable, in the foreground, and reacting to or illustrating the commercial message.

When the second use cycle begins, both schedules start all over again with the original use of the No. 1 payment. A moderate campaign—let us say, twenty-six uses in each thirteen-week cycle—would net the on-camera performer $2,001.25 per cycle, or $8,005.00 a year. Twenty-six uses per cycle off camera would amount to $1,535.75 per cycle, or $6,143.00 per year.

The actor recording a commercial receives $300.00 or $225.60, whichever is applicable, no matter *where in the country the commercial is made*, if made under a SAG or AFTRA contract. Use payments, however, vary with city and area covered. Wild spots pay the initial recording fees nationwide, but their payments differ widely, again depending on the cities where the commercial is played. A complete schedule of payments along with the contract provisions that protect the performer would fill a book by themselves. The preceding breakdown gives you some idea of what you might expect to make, and a little arithmetic will show you that with a large number of uses per cycle, the yearly return can be very substantial—and, of course, we are talking about a *single* commercial. When called to do a commercial you have a right to know where the commercial will play. If it is made under a union jurisdiction, check with your local union office for information as to the payment you can expect to receive.

Extras

Some actors supplement their income by doing extra work in commercials. Extras are background players who fill out the scene. To do extra work in most commercials you must be a member of SAG, and you cannot break into SAG by being cast as an extra. Extras are cast by the ad agencies or production houses, and if you wish to be considered for employment in this area, you should so state on your résumé. Many actors feel that they would be type-cast if they indicated they would accept extra employment. It is difficult to advise the newcomer as to his course of action, but in general it is a good idea to get established as a principal player *first* and *then* consider taking extra work. (For a schedule of payment for extras, contact your local union office.)

Upgrading of Extras

An actor may be called to do extra work and then in the course of the filming be "upgraded." A director may pick an actor to do a piece of business which has not been previously indicated in the shooting script. If the actor is now identifiable, in the foreground, and is reacting to or illustrating the commercial message, he or she is then upgraded to a principal and is entitled to be paid as a principal for his or her day's work and to all residual payments. Occasionally in the editing, an actor's performance upgrades him to a principal. For the above reasons some actors are willing to perform as extras when told in advance that there is a possibility of their being upgraded.

Conversely, sad to say, a principal may end as "the face on the cutting-room floor," or because of the editing, his or her performance may be classified as that of an extra. The actor still gets pay as a principal for the day's work but will receive no residuals. The only protection an actor has against being downgraded is a previous written agreement to receive an established amount of money for a thirteen-week (or longer) period. This is very difficult to negotiate, but if you should get such a contract you probably won't be cut out of the commercial!

Commercials Produced for Cable Transmission Only

In the negotiations concluded in February 1982, for the first time SAG and AFTRA established contract coverage for performers working on commercials made directly for cable transmission. Since cable systems and cable programming are proliferating at a fast rate, these contract terms could in a very short time greatly increase the incomes of TV performers.

Unlike commercials made for broadcast TV, where a session fee must be paid for each commercial made within the session period, the producer of cable commercials is allowed to make multiple commercials within a production day, both for on-camera commercials and the two-hour session for voice-overs, and pay for them at a lesser fee.

Schedule of payments
Principals

On-camera day rate		Off-camera session fee	
First commercial	$300.00	First commercial	$225.60
Each additional commercial	$100.00	Each additional commercial	$ 72.50

table p. 277

Use Payment

On-camera day rate		Off-camera session fee	
4-week period	$100.00	4-week period	$ 75.00
13-week period	$300.00	13-week period	$225.00
52-week period	$750.00	52-week period	$564.00

For rates for commercials made for broadcast TV and played on cable, check your local union office.

Payments for Industrials

The actor working under an industrial contract gets paid $225 for a day's work or, if hired for five days, $789. For voice-over he or she is paid $175 for a four-hour session. This covers the payment for ten minutes of footage. For each additional ten minutes of footage recorded within the four-hour span the actor is paid $70. A new session does not begin if the recording takes more than four hours. Instead the actor is paid overtime.

Pension and Welfare

Both AFTRA and SAG have pension and welfare plans funded by the contractual sums of money contributed by the employers to plans (in addition to the actor's salary) each time the actor works under union jurisdiction. For the amount of money an actor must make to qualify for benefits, contact your local union office.

Radio Commercials Payment

A radio commercial session fee pays $110 no matter where in the country the commercial is made, if under an AFTRA contract. The wild spot (this is the most common radio use) is paid for according to the cities in which they are used. A thirteen-week unlimited use in New York, Chicago, and Los Angeles would pay $278. By adding additional cities, the performer could earn $400 to $500 or even more. Network program use pays much more, as does use on a regional network. These latter categories are used much less frequently by advertisers. For their rates consult your local AFTRA office.

The Taft-Hartley Act

The Taft-Hartley Act makes it illegal to deny employment to an individual solely because he does not belong to a union, but this does not mean that doors are open to everyone. In actual practice, this labor law does little for the performer who is trying to break into the business. It does permit an actor to work for thirty consecutive working days (six weeks) without having to join a union. But most actors *want* to join a union—AFTRA or SAG or both. The one advantage of the Taft-Hartley Act to the actor breaking in is that the pay which he or she receives for nonunion work during the six-week period may help toward the payment of union initiation fees and dues. If, for instance, an actor were fortunate enough to get several calls for extra work on a soap opera, the money earned would be enough to join AFTRA, and the actor would have taken the first step toward getting into SAG.

Your Child and Commercials: Home Training

We said earlier that your child might be selected for a commercial even though you were not. That is true, but not of the untrained child. The proud mother is apt to say, "My little girl is so cute she just ought to be in commercials." But that cute little girl has to be able to read for an agent or caster with all the assurance of a grown-up. She has to keep her composure on the set, endure long hours of shooting, or what is almost worse, endure the endless and dull hours spent sitting around while lighting is changed and cameras are moved for the various shots.

So let's begin at the beginning—with that cute little girl. What attributes should she have? Right off, she doesn't have to be beautiful, but she should have a personality that shines. She should be bright and gregarious—that is, she should like people and not be shy about meeting with them and talking to them. If she is a show-off, fine, although that may sometimes present problems that we'll discuss later. She should be a good reader, and it is a big plus if she likes to act, perhaps in children's plays at school.

Work with your child at home. Help her in her reading on a regular schedule—make it part of her homework, but don't let her think of it as homework. Get children's plays from the library and read with her. To further her interest in commercials, comment on TV commercials that have children in them. Say, "You could do that." Tape commercials from TV on your cassette recorder. Have your child do them, and play them back. There is a fascination to most children in hearing themselves on a cassette.

If your child has trouble making the reading of the actual copy sound natural, ask, "How would you say it?" When the child has paraphrased a line and rendered a natural reading, return to the original line. Maybe now he or she can make *that* line sound natural. Even in the final shooting of the commercial, producers have been known to change a line somewhat so it will come out naturally. But, of course, your aim is to get a natural reading from your child without changing the copy.

Make up commercials—about your breakfast food, soft drinks, candy—anything. Make a game of it. Make it fun—not a conscious preparation for that audition that could mean so much. Get the child to give unself-conscious reactions to products: a great big smile after a bowl of Quaker Oats or a drink of Coke.

If your child is a show-off, your problem may be in getting him or her to listen long enough to take direction. Show-offs are so anxious to start performing they don't want to take the time to listen carefully. Make a game of remembering. Write a list of your directions as you give them, and then check off the ones the child got right when performing. Make a big point of the fact that it will be of paramount importance in a real situation to remember and follow directions. Remember, the show-off is most likely the one who most *wants* to do commercials.

If your child is at the prereading age, follow many of the above steps, such as playing at reacting to the product—a big smile, and then simple vocal reactions, such as "Mmm, good!" or "Mommy, this tastes great!" A reaction that is real and not self-conscious may be just enough to win an audition.

Above all, don't force your child, don't become impatient or short-tempered. Make it a game—make it fun. If it isn't fun, you may soon find a big psychological block erected by your child that will turn him or her off completely, and you may never be able to restimulate that initial interest.

TV Commercial Schools

This has been designed as a "do it yourself" primer. We have attempted to be as thorough as possible in pointing out areas of employment, particularly in the field of commercials. We have outlined the steps to take to get work and to train yourself at home to become an effective commercial performer. We would, however, be negligent if we did not mention that TV schools exist—places where you can see yourself in video playback as you practice under the instruction of excellent teachers who are themselves highly successful commercial performers.

The only national school is the Weist-Barron School. It is based in New York, has been turning out highly successful performers for twenty five years, and its branches have been listed earlier in this book. Its classes are considered by agents to be by far the best available. If you think of the modest investment it takes to enroll and the possible returns on your investment, you will want to take advantage of the opportunity to sharpen your talents. In New York, before you enroll you are invited to audit a commercial class free. The school is located at 35 West 45th Street, in Manhattan. A brochure and schedule of all classes will be mailed upon request. In addition to the commercial course there are also classes in soap-opera acting and for children.

In our earlier discussion of agents and how to get to know them you no doubt noted that the task was not easy. Weist-Barron pioneered the practice of having agents visit classes to meet the students and see them perform, thus giving the students the opportunity of "showing their wares," and the agents the chance to discover new talent to send out on auditions. The student met the agent at the *end* of the course, when the students training had readied him or her for the exposure.

This is still the practice at Weist-Barron and will continue to be. There are many TV schools in New York, and you will find ads for them in *Backstage*. Some are quite good. The uninitiated, however, should be warned about the schools that offer you the opportunity of meeting an agent before you have had sufficient training to give your best performance. An audition for an agent that is not an excellent audition is worse than none at all. You will be paying for an agent to say to himself, "Well, I can cross that actor off my list."

Also, actors should beware of schools that promise to make them successful commercial performers "overnight." Be sure you pick the right school, visit them all, observe the classes (if the school will not permit you to audit a class, beware!), check out the studios and the video equipment. Do they have color? A TelePrompTer? A textbook with clearly outlined lessons? How do prices compare? Then make your decision. Whether it be Weist-Barron or any of the others—study. In the field of commercials it is impossible to be overtrained.

The Voice-over Showcase

Getting a hearing of your voice-over tape is not easy. Although the *Ross Report* lists the agents who have reel-to-reel playback equipment, agents are so busy that they just do not have the time to listen to all the tapes submitted to them. If you are new in the business and not well known by agents, your tape may be stacked with many others in a corner of the office and not be heard for a year or more, if ever.

To make sure your tape gets a hearing, Weist-Barron holds a tape clinic twice a year, called the Voice-over Showcase. Ten agents and/ or ad agency casting directors in ten separate sessions listen to your tape and criticize it. Or you may bring two tapes and get a comparison opinion from the agent. Anyone may enroll, but a preliminary judgment will be made by the school as to the advisability of your joining the course. A tape substandard in production quality, or one that does not show you off to advantage is a poor introduction to those who might help you gain employment in the voice-over field.

The Name of the Game

A cliché? Yes. But an appropriately omnibus one. It includes many aspects of the subject being discussed. Because the phrase is so often used and we all know what it means, let's proceed with the name of the game in commercials.

First, the name of the game is *energy*. You must exude energy at all times—at the audition, at the shooting. No one is going to buy your product—they're not even going to listen to you—if you talk to them in a matter-of-fact way. If you don't show enough enthusiasm in your sell to prove how well you like the product, the effect is that you just don't care whether they buy it or not.

Energy does not mean shouting. It means involvement. It means displaying a belief in what you are saying. Have you ever been at a cocktail party where someone is engaging you in conversation so energetically that you can hardly get away even though you'd like to? You stand there with your empty glass in hand dying for another drink, but you can't break away. If you can capture that kind of energy, that kind of involvement in your delivery of commercials, you're off and running.

Second, the name of the game is *confidence*. Confidence breeds confidence. When you exude confidence, you make your auditioner feel confident that you could deliver a good commercial if you were chosen for the part. Confidence, your belief in yourself, radiates to the auditioner. You're acting like a winner, and everyone wants to go with a winner.

Third, the name of the game is *taking rejection*. You can't win all the time. Because competition is keen and the woods are full of good performers, you're not going to make it every time. If you know that you gave a really good audition, the reason you didn't win could be because someone else was considered a better type—and don't discount the fact that he or she may have given a better reading. So dry your tears and on to the next audition. To paraphrase Lincoln, you can be rejected by some of the people all of the time, and all of the people some of the time, but you can't be rejected by all of the people all of the time.

Fourth, the name of the game is *numbers*. Most people have to go to a number of auditions to get one job. Oh, sure, some people have landed a commercial the first time out. We call this "a hole in one." Take into account the law of averages. If thirty people were to be called for every audition (and, of course, the number varies), your percentage of wins would be one in thirty. It is the purpose of this book to increase your percentage of wins.

Fifth, the name of the game is *likability*. You are more apt to be hired if people like you. You must have or must develop an engaging personality. Don't let nerves or shyness overcome you. If you are taciturn, if you never smile, and behave like a walking statue, you have one mark against you before you even audition. And how many times have you seen the stone faces on Mount Rushmore used in commercials?

Sixth, the name of the game is *opinion*. Everyone has a different opinion about you—your appearance, your abilities. One will say, "She'll never work." Another will think you're "wonderful." Nowhere in the field are there more opinions formed than by photographs. One agent will look at a photo and say, "This is a terrific photo. You'll get a lot of work with this picture." Another will look at the same picture and say, "This is a picture of you? When was it taken? You need new pictures!" Don't be discouraged by this. It is normal in the business. Regardless of what you hear from others, you have to have the confidence to believe that what you think is right, is right!

But abide by the majority opinion. In this business, as in all others, there will always be a minority opinion. Why not? Everyone has different ideas about everything.

Seventh, the name of the game is *persistence*. Success rarely happens overnight. "If at first you don't succeed . . . " You know the rest. Keep making the rounds, making contacts, sending out pictures and postcards, and don't let your morale sag. If New York is your target, be sure you come with enough money to last you for a couple of years, or as many actors do, get a part-time job to help finance your career. If you have superior talent, someday you should make it, so KEEP AT IT, KEEP AT IT, KEEP AT IT.

Appendix

Practice Commercials

SAFEST

VIDEO	AUDIO
FADE IN ON HIGH-FASHION MODEL AND OUTDOORS WOMAN WITH PLANT STANDING IN LIMBO. MAN LOOKS AT EACH OF THEM AND TALKS TO CAMERA, REFERRING TO THEM.	MAN: One of these women is cleaner than the other, but it's not the one you think.
CUT TO CLOSE-UP OF MODEL	Because the real problem in getting clean is the dirt you can't see: odor-causing bacteria.
CUT BACK TO OUTDOORS WOMAN	This woman is cleaner because she uses Safe-est.
DISSOLVE TO PRODUCT BEING USED BY WOMAN IN SHOWER	Safe-est is effective against odor-causing bacteria, the dirt you can't see.
DISSOLVE TO PACKAGE SHOT	MAN (V/O): Safe-est . . .
SUPER OVER PACKAGE SHOT	MAN (V/O): (READING SUPER): For the dirt that causes odor, the dirt you can't see.

FAX

VIDEO	AUDIO
OPEN ON VARIOUS SHOTS OF FAMILY PLAYING FOOTBALL.	MOTHER (O.C.): Well, nobody ever said that football was the cleanest game in the world.
CAMERA PULLS BACK AS MOTHER IS PUTTING CLOTHES IN WASHER. BOX OF FAX IS ON TOP OF MACHINE. SHE IS HOLDING DIRTY FOOTBALL JERSEY, WHICH SHE TOSSES INTO MACHINE.	But this team of mine . . . and their daddy . . . must get extra points for dirty clothes. Just look . . . mud and dirt from head to toe . . . perspirey, too! What fantastic luck I found Fax . . . with real borax. Fax gets everything a new kind of clean . . . you want to get close to.

Arnie's Homestyle White Bread

These days, it seems hardly anything is made very well. That's why David and I started making things ourselves. He built these cupboards, I made these preserves—I even started baking bread. 'Course, I can't do that very often, so mostly I buy this: Arnie's Homestyle White Bread. In the big, two-pound size. It's not just the best bread you can buy; it's the best value. You know, I discovered that the two-pound Arnie's Homestyle White Bread costs only a bit more than ordinary white bread? [Pats bread.] My kind of people.

Barry's

WOMAN (on camera):

If you work, you know how tough it is to go home and start cooking. I've been working for years, so I've learned a few secrets. Any time I don't feel like cooking, I let Barry's help me out. They make so many good things . . . turkey tetrazzini, shrimp and lobster newburg, creamed chicken, and lots more.

I worked hard today—but thanks to Barry's—I'm not cooking tonight.

Scotch Flow Gold

WOMAN:

Beautiful wood just makes this room. Believe me, it hasn't always looked like this. I tried covering it up with wax. And then I discovered Scotch Flow Gold. Flow Gold cleaned and conditioned the wood, brought out the color and contrast. It penetrated the wood, and that dry, faded look seemed to disappear, as well as scratches. A nice thing about Flow Gold is it doesn't attract dust. Makes my job a lot easier. After seeing what Flow Gold can do, use it weekly. And keep it that way . . . And there's the large size for the big jobs.

Med-I-Res

On Camera—Stand-up Audition

ANNOUNCER:

[Over] Once upon a time—quite recently—Med-I-Res decided to make a new kind of adhesive tape.

Since no two skins are alike,

they decided to make it invisible . . .

to make tape that actually looks—and acts like your skin!

And they decided to put this new tape in an extra-hard dispenser [flip—snip]

Med-I-Res is sure you'll find this new tape right for all your bandaging. Band-It Clear Tape.

That's the name . . . Band-It Clear Tape.

Try it.
You will like it.

Nationwide Airlines
MALE/FEMALE ANNOUNCER:
Florida is warm, sunny, relaxing, exciting—everything but boring, except for the trip down. I came down on the airline with no movies—two and a half hours of looking out the window. I'm going back on Nationwide, the airline with movies in every section of every wide-cabin plane. It's your vacation, so why be bored on an airline with no movies when you can say: "Nationwide Airlines, take me, I'm yours."?

Commonly Mispronounced Words

Congratulations	*congratulations, not congradulations*
education	*ed-U-cation, not ed-ja-cation*
electric	*el-ectric, not ah-lectric nor ee-lectric*
era	*ear-ah, not error*
for	*for, not fer nor fir*
get	*not git*
gasoline	*gass-o-line, not gaz-o-line*
greasy	*greesie, not greezie*
grocers	*not groshers*
I	*eye-ee, not ah*
just	*not jest nor jist*
length	*lengk-th, not lenth*
mirror	*mir-rer, not mir*
new	*n-eu-w, not noo*
often	*offen, not off-ten*
perspiration	*pers-per-a-shun, not press-per-a-shun*
protects	*use a KTS sound, not a TEX sound*
strength	*strenk-th, not strenth*

Put "er" endings on words ending in "er" (however, not howevah)
Put "a" endings on words ending in "a" (Ada, not Ader)
The han-ging "g" must go! (go-ing, not going-guh)
Don't dentalize your ts. It's hunt-er, not hun-ter; dent-ist, not dentist; lat-er, not la-ter.

Enunciation Exercises

Exaggerate the use of the lips without uttering a sound and have others try to guess what is being said.

For articulation, the following tongue twisters make excellent practice until the entire exercise can be read without error in thirty seconds.

1. Amos Ames, the amiable aeronaut, aided in an aerial enterprise at the age of eighty-eight.
2. Some shun sunshine. Do you shun sunshine?
3. Fine white wine vinegar with veal.
4. Bring a bit of buttered brown bran bread.
5. Geese cackle, cattle low, crows caw, cocks crow.
6. Eight gray geese in a green field gazing.
7. Six thick thistle sticks.
8. Lucy likes light literature.
9. A big black bug bit a big black bear.
10. Peter Prangle, the prickly prangly pear picker, picked three pecks of prickly prangly pears from the prickly prangly pear trees on the pleasant prairies.
11. Theophilus Thistle, the successful thistle sifter, in sifting a sieveful of unsifted thistles, thrust three thousand thistles through the thick of his thumb. Now, if Theophilus Thistle, the successful thistle sifter in sifting a sieveful of unsifted thistles, thrust three thousand thistles though the thick of his thumb, see that thou, in sifting a sieveful of unsifted thistles, thrust not three thousand thistles through the thick of thy thumb. Success to the successful thistle sifter.

When you are doing your enunciation exercises watch yourself in the mirror to be sure you are moving your lips. Some people habitually speak as if they were practicing to be a ventriloquist. Three things result. First, their enunciation is often sloppy. Second, because the mouth is hardly opening, they are bottling up the sound that should be coming forth. You may have a very good voice, but no one will know it unless you let it out. Last, a large part of the face's activity that you should be projecting comes from the movement of the lips. If you are in the habit of not moving your lips, you will feel awkward at first as you make your lips really move, but as you watch yourself in the mirror you will see that it does not *look* awkward. Exaggerate the movement gradually until it looks natural.

Glossary

(The words in quotes are usually spoken directions to you.)

"Action"	Begin the action for this scene.
A.D.	The assistant director. You report to him or her upon arrival at the film set.
Ad agency producer (TVCP)	The person from the ad agency in overall charge of producing a commercial.
AFTRA	American Federation of Television and Radio Artists. The actors' union governing audiotape and videotape productions.
Agent	A person who sends actors on auditions and receives a percentage (10 percent) of the actor's pay.
Animation	Action produced by photographing sequential drawings.
Call-back	Second summons to audition received by actors not eliminated in the first audition.
Call sheet	A list, usually mimeographed, showing times and dates actors and crews are to report to work.
Camera angle	The angle at which the camera and lens "view" the scene to be shot.
Casting director	Someone who casts commercials for an advertising agency or film company. The casting director often works through agents in getting actors for auditions.
Clapstick	A device used to synchronize the sound with the picture.
Close shot	A scene in which the object being photographed is shown in full, without extraneous material around it. A man shown head-to-toe

	would be a close shot. A shot of the nose and cheek of a face would be another.
Closed set	A room interior.
Close-up (C.U.), medium close-up (M.C.U.), extreme close-up (E.C.U.)	Any section of a close shot.
"Cut" (director)	Stop camera, actors stop action.
Direct recording	Recording sounds directly on film in synchronization with the action.
Dissolve	Fading out of the scene as another fades in. Can be timed to various sequential lengths: one foot, then two feet, then three feet, etc.
Dolly shot	A scene in which the camera, mounted on a moving tripod, moves either closer to or farther from the object being photographed.
Dubbing	Matching words against the lip movement of a silent picture.
DV	Direct voice; on-camera pitch.
Gaff or gaffer	An electrician.
Grip	A stagehand.
Horn	A sound speaker.
Independent casting director	A member of a company who performs the casting function for an ad agency.
"In the can"	The film is finished.
"Let's make a safety"	"We need a protection take," or "Will somebody please make a decision here?"
Limbo	Seamless paper background for a shot.
Live action	Shooting actual people or things rather than animation or still artwork.
Location	Any site away from the studio, either interior or exterior.
Logo	The client's emblem (for example, the camel of Camel cigarettes).
Long shot (L.S.), medium long shot (M.L.S.)	A scene that establishes the general location of the total action, such as a shot of Times Square.

Matte shot	A shot made by masking out parts of a scene when originally taking the picture. Blue backing (called U.V.) is replacing this process.
Medium shot (M.S.)	A scene that concentrates on the significant portion of a long shot—the front of the Palace Theater on Times Square, for instance.
Montage	The combining of several shots to make up a multifaceted picture on the screen. (This is the American version of the montage; the European version is somewhat different.)
MOT	A silent scene, without dialogue ("mit 'out" sound).
O.C.	On camera—that is, the actor is seen and heard on camera.
"On bells" (director)	Silence on the set, we are recording sound!
Pan shot (pan right, pan left)	A scene in which the camera is moved in order to follow the significant action.
Pot, the	An engineer's monitor board.
"Print it" (director)	A good take; one to be used.
Process shot	A shot in which the background is photographically produced by a projector running in synchronization with the actual taking camera.
Production company	A film company that actually shoots the commercial. They vary in size from one person with no studio to large companies with fifty to a hundred employees as well as studios and other expensive facilities.
Props	Anything on the set that is not people or part of the set itself, such as furniture, vases, pictures, etc. Also, the nickname of the property manager.
SAG	Screen Actors Guild, a trade union to which all film actors must belong.
Shot	A piece of action as taken by the camera.
Slate (bottom portion of the clapstick)	A device on which is recorded the number of each scene and each take. It is photographed at the head of each scene, so that the scene

	can be identified. Also, the performer's introductory identification at an audition.
Sound man, sound technician	The man (or woman) who records the dialogue.
"Speed" (sound technician, camera operator)	The word that lets the director know that film and tape are up to recording speed.
Split screen	An optical effect whereby two diverse elements appear on the screen simultaneously.
Stage manager	The person in charge of the procedure of the production and to whom you will report upon arrival at the video set.
Storyboard	A series of drawings from the key scenes of a film to guide the director, scene designer, cameraperson, etc.
"Strike it"	Remove it from the scene.
Super	To superimpose something on the screen.
Take	A single version of an action that has been photographed. "Scene one, take one"; "Scene one, take two." The best "take" of each scene is the one finally used.
Talent, the	The actor or actress.
Track	A section of the film that carries the sound portion.
Tripod	The instrument on which the camera is mounted.
Voice-over (V.O.)	An off-screen narration, as distinguished from lip sync. Lip sync is sometimes called "direct voice" or "D.V."
Wipe	An optical effect in which one picture seems to push another off the screen.
Zoom shot	A scene in which the image appears to move toward or away from the camera. It requires a special lens. Not to be confused with dolly shot, where the whole camera actually moves.

Index